THE
MUTUAL
FUND
TRAP

THE
MUTUAL
FUND
TRAP

John L. Springer

HENRY REGNERY COMPANY•CHICAGO

Published by Henry Regnery Company
114 West Illinois Street, Chicago, Illinois 60610

Manufactured in the United States of America
Library of Congress Catalog Card Number: 72-80941

Contents

THE MUTUAL FUND TRAP

1

Mutual Funds: Everybody's Way to Get Rich?

PERHAPS at no time in our history — certainly never in the memory of living men — has it been more difficult for the American investor to decide how to protect savings and to make them grow.

Not long ago, if you sought to maintain the value of your money, financial advisers could safely suggest that you place it in a savings account where it would draw a secure, if modest, rate of return. You could reasonably expect to offset both low taxes payable upon the interest and any decrease in its purchasing power due to inflation. Thus during the early 1930s, when living costs actually declined, the purchasing power of dollars in a savings account could even increase. Sophisticated investors, like pension fund managers, could achieve reasonably satisfactory returns by investing in utility bonds of such industrial giants as General Motors, American Telephone and Telegraph, and General Electric. Investing in stocks was left for the relatively few — those with sufficient skills (or foolhardiness)

1

to venture among the bulls and bears of Wall Street or with fortunes large enough to hire others to venture for them.

It was generally recognized that investing in common stocks was mainly a speculative endeavor; like the racetrack, Wall Street was a place where huge sums could be made or lost in a thrice. According to the prevailing view, buying and selling common stocks was only for those who could afford to lose their entire stake. In the thirties, after the wild market crash in which prices of many common stocks dropped to 5 percent of their former highs, the idea that such stocks were safe was as popular as the idea that the earth was flat.

Where Can You Put Your Money?

The picture has changed. If you now have savings, you first face an involved question about where to put your dollars to make sure that they will buy at least as much for you in the future as they do today. Many financial advisers no longer recommend long-term deposits in savings accounts or U.S. government savings bonds. Some even discourage investments in the gilt-edged bonds of the General Motors and General Electrics. Their red light on fixed-income investments is based upon the expectation (which seems universal) that inflation will be a world problem for years, if not forever. Even people who say we are making progress against inflation don't say that the trend toward higher living costs is being reversed. They say that the trend may not be as bad as it was — it may be trimmed from its recent 5 percent per year to a "more moderate" 3 or 4 percent.

Thus, the average person who puts money where he or she will get a fixed dollar return in the future *must* draw at least 6.5 percent interest merely to offset the decreased purchasing power due to inflation. The person will need 2.5 percent to cover the average taxes that the government exacts on interest and 4 percent more to offset the "moderate" inflation rate. Six and one-half percent interest is more than savings institutions and government savings bonds have been paying. Thus the prudent saver must turn to other bonds. If the saver finds a safe one paying 7 percent, the saver will have — after paying 30 percent taxes on this interest and 4 percent inflation — a true return of 0.9 percent per year on the money.

If you want your money to make money, you must look elsewhere. Capitalizing on growing public disenchantment with fixed-income savings and investments, promoters have seen to it that there is no dearth of investment "opportunities." The common stock markets themselves have been a prime beneficiary of this search. Some 32 million Americans are now listed as direct shareholders in American businesses — double the number of little more than a decade ago. Competing for your investment dollar are such vehicles as real estate trusts, syndicated oil and mineral extraction companies, syndicates to invest in cattle, fine art, airplanes to be leased to airliners, and "venture capital" pools to gamble that promising small companies will become rich big ones. Insurance companies and commercial banks are constantly offering schemes — annuities, pension programs — to bring investors' funds under their management.

The "Success Story" of the Century

Without a doubt, the most successful scheme has been that of the investment companies that are popularly known as mutual funds. The fund idea is based upon a double premise: that the typical investor lacks the interest, talent, or time to manage investment affairs successfully; and that greater safety lies in diversification — spreading capital among many enterprises — and that the individual investor lacks the money to diversify effectively.

For example, in order to buy 100 shares in each corporation represented in the typical mutual fund portfolio, the individual would require at least $100,000. (To buy fewer than 100 shares would be economically unwise. In each such "odd-lot" trans-action the investor would pay at least one-eighth of a point per share and receive at least one-eighth of a point less when the shares were sold, plus a stock exchange surcharge and perhaps the frustration of engaging in a Diogenes-like search for a broker willing to execute orders.)

Mutual fund promoters represent that for the typical in-dividual, who lacks the training and experience to invest prudently and the money to diversify successfully, they provide professional management capable of doing precisely that. They claim they can achieve better overall results than most people can get on their own. Although some funds invest solely in such fixed-income securities as bonds, and others balance their portfolio between bonds and preferred stocks for "safety" and common stocks for "growth," most mutual funds invest most heavily in common stocks. By doing so they claim to provide a hedge against inflation and the decreased purchasing power of the dollar.

That mutual funds have done a masterful job of selling themselves to the public — until recently, at least — cannot be denied. In fact, their growth has been the most amazing investment accomplishment of the century.

According to the Investment Company Institute, a trade organization comprising most major funds, at the end of 1940 there were 68 mutual funds with a total of 296,000 accounts and assets of $448 million. Comparable figures at the end of 1970 were 361 funds, 11 million accounts, and total assets of $47.6 billion. In the latter year, owners of mutual funds accounted for 27.4 percent of the total shareowners in the United States. They accounted for 46.2 percent of the individuals who owned shares listed on the New York Stock Exchange.

It is significant to note that the funds have been more successful in selling their shares to women than to men. Fifty-two percent of mutual fund owners are women, whereas men outnumber women as direct owners of shares in public corporations by a margin of 50.9 percent to 49.1 percent.

The funds also have been more successful in the Pacific and North Central states than elsewhere. On the West Coast mutual fund shareowners represent 38.1 percent of the total of all shareowners of all kinds of securities, while in the Middle Atlantic and South Central states the corresponding figures are only 23.3 and 21.4 percent, respectively. If there is a "dream territory" for mutual fund salespeople, it is the Anaheim, Santa Ana, and Garden Grove sections of California, where 51.3 percent of all shareowners are fund owners, and in San Diego, where 49 of every 100 shareowners of all types hold fund shares. In contrast, of every 100 shareholders in Houston, Texas, only 13.7 — fewer than one in seven — use a fund.[1]

In line with the increasing clout of the funds, the volume of institutional trading rose spectacularly during the 1960s. In

1960 mutual funds were responsible for transactions involving 71 million shares on the New York Stock Exchange — roughly 5.5 percent of the total traded by all investors except members of the Exchange. By 1969 the estimated total volume of shares traded by the funds had increased more than eight times, 584 million shares, and funds accounted for 12.9 percent of all nonmember trading on the Exchange.

More recently it has been estimated that institutional investors account for well over 50 percent of all transactions on the New York Stock Exchange. These professionals manage the portfolios of pension funds, bank and bank trusts, university endowment funds, and mutual funds. In contrast, in the wild stock-trading days of 1928 and 1929 it was estimated that institutions were responsible for only one trade in twenty.

The funds have confounded — and converted — many distinguished doubters. One of the strongest bastions against funds was Merrill Lynch, Pierce, Fenner and Smith, the world's largest brokerage house. For years Merrill Lynch argued that it could provide investment suggestions that would enable its customers to achieve better results than they could get by buying funds. In 1970, however, Merrill Lynch decided to go over to the enemy. It has since underwritten funds. At a National Press Club conference on September 15, 1970, a reporter asked the firm's president, Donald T. Regan, what prompted the decision. "This was a decision of our customers," Regan replied. "In a survey, we found that 30 percent of our customers already owned mutual funds and had had to go somewhere else to buy them. So we felt we had to get back to the head of the parade and a position of leadership with our own customers."

Another group of doubters was made up of insurance companies. "If there is one sentence I'd pay a thousand dollars never to hear again," a life insurance agent once told me, "it's the expression, 'buy term and invest the rest.'" He was referring to the success of fund salespeople in convincing holders of life insurance policies with cash-surrender values that they could achieve better results by cashing in their policies, buying an equivalent amount of term insurance without immediate cash value, and using the cash received and savings on premium payments to buy fund shares. Since the cash-surrender value in insurance policies earned 3 percent a year while many funds could cite annual increases of 10 percent in share value, this message had a dramatic appeal. From 1950 to 1970 the ratio of cash-value insurance to total savings fell steadily. At the end of the period barely 20 percent of Americans' savings went into insurance, as opposed to 42 percent two decades before. Funds and other investment companies increased their share of savings more than threefold, going from 2.5 to 8 percent. While total life insurance assets merely tripled during the period, fund assets increased more than 20 times, going from $2.5 billion in 1950 to $55 billion in 1970.

The significance of these figures was not lost on the companies. Insurance companies began a stampede to start or buy funds of their own; by 1971 some 70 funds were found to be affiliated with insurance institutions. Some observers have predicted that in the future almost all big funds will have such a tie-in. The incentive for this affiliation rests on the massive scale of the insurance companies' marketing operation. In 1970, according to the Institute of Life Insurance, there were 450,000 insurance salespeople working full- or part-time in the United States, some two and one-half times the brokers and salespeople licensed to sell mutual funds. Moreover, insurance salespeople have contacts with all classes of the population, including millions of lower-income people who might be persuaded to take their money out of savings accounts and into funds with exciting prospects for big profits. Some observers have speculated that if insurance salespeople were trained to sell funds and turned loose on the 9 out of 10 Americans who now own no fund shares, they would soon have a stranglehold on the business.

These predictions seemed all the more realistic in 1970 when Sears, Roebuck and Company, by all odds the nation's largest retail establishment, with firm roots in every section of the country, began putting its resources behind the Allstate Enterprises Stock Fund. With 820 stores equipped to sell shares over the counter, Sears was expected by some observers to zoom into the front ranks of the funds immediately. So far that has not happened. After one year of intensive promotion Allstate Enterprises had a disappointing 88,000 shareholders — an average of 100 per store — and total net assets of $144,440,000. Nor has Allstate's investment performance caused its competitors any heartburn. In one year, when the Dow-Jones Industrial Average gained 16.7 percent (going from 753 to 879) Allstate chalked up a relatively mediocre 10 percent gain (8.3 in asset value, 1.7 in dividends).

Reports from other insurance companies — John Hancock, Mutual of New York, CNA — were equally gloomy. One unexpected irony: life insurance salespeople had been trained to belittle mutual funds and to extol the "safety of principal" to be found in a life insurance policy that built cash values year by year. They had been taught to tell prospective buyers that fund investments could produce ruinous losses, and as they began to sell fund shares in the bear market of 1969 and 1970, they discovered that they had been right about mutual funds all the time. CNA's experience was particularly distressing. It bought the Manhattan Fund from Gerald Tsai, one of the industry's glamour portfolio managers in the mid-sixties, and then watched as redemptions due to the fund's poor performance in a bear market cut its assets in half.

Is It True What They Say about Mutual Funds?

Concurrent with this dynamic growth — except recently, about which more later — many notions about mutual funds have become widely accepted. Around the funds, for example, has grown the mystique of "professional management," the belief that those who handle fund portfolios are a breed apart from the rest of us, with information and insights we can merely envy. Fund salespeople have painted a picture of almost automatic riches for the average American — put $50 per month into fund shares and buy a yacht in 20 years. One promoter tells prospective buyers that "mutual funds are the *only* investment for the average person who wants to make capital grow," and many of the prospects believe it.

But the public has been told only one part of the mutual fund story, the part that the funds want to tell. With their vast sales apparatus they inundate millions of individual investors annually with arguments that seem reasonable on their face and for which the prospective client lacks facts and figures to counteract. With their huge advertising appropriations they bombard the public with the viewpoint that "professionals know best." They gain ready access to the financial press, where their opinions and forecasts — however erroneous — are reproduced uncritically. The record needs to be examined critically, apart from fund propaganda.

Is it true what they say about mutual funds? How much veracity lies in the claim that they are the ideal investment medium for the individual investor?

What is their *real* performance record in bull and bear markets?

Are they managed primarily to benefit the shareholder — or to line the pockets of their promoters?

How much does the shareholder really pay to have money managed?

Does the fund salesperson's service merit the commission, or does he or she often render an absolute disservice and take money that could be invested elsewhere? Can the salesperson be trusted to give truly disinterested advice?

What about "no-loads," the funds that can be bought without payment of a sales commission? Are they as risky as some fund salespeople imply?

Where can a prospective purchaser find honest investment advice from sources with no axes to grind? What are the major pitfalls to avoid in choosing a fund? Is there a certain "best time in the year" to buy?

These and other essential questions about mutual funds will be answered in the pages that follow.

2

"You Name It — We've Got It"

Mutual funds have grown spectacularly in number of shareholders and total assets because they have notably fulfilled the tested prescription for success: find a need and fill it. Millions of persons obviously need and want someone to manage their investments. When this need is combined with the shrewd selling of promises, the lure of the professionally managed fund that will make them rich is difficult for millions to resist.

The fund industry has responded in a remarkable way to the needs, preexisting or created, of the investing public. No matter what your investment preference, you probably can find a fund to provide it. You can find funds that are baroquely conservative and others that are wildly speculative, funds that seek to protect your dollars above all and funds that look for volatile high fliers that will double your money in a month.

Mutual funds by and large fall into five basic categories:

Balanced funds take the position that the future is hardly

9

predictable and that the best procedure is to invest some money in common stocks and some in bonds and preferred stocks. Balanced funds seek to maintain certain levels of speculative and conservative common stocks and different classes of fixed-income securities. If the stock market goes up, the common stock part of the portfolio will rise with it. If the market goes down, the "defensive" part of the portfolio, the bonds and preferred stock, will produce income and shield shareholders against serious losses. Although it is not admitted, the investment posture of balanced funds belies the argument that investment managers have superior ability to foretell market trends. What they are saying essentially is that they do not know what the market will do. Therefore, they seek to avoid loss no matter what happens.

Income funds strive for good dividend or interest income through investments in bonds and preferred stocks. Although they are somewhat out of favor with common stock investors (who are increasingly tax-conscious and seek capital gains, which are taxed at lower rates and often at a time of the shareholders' own choosing), they have become more popular with persons seeking current income — generally the retired or well-to-do without salaries or wages. This group has turned to bonds and debentures, which give substantially greater returns. In 1972, for instance, one could get twice as much income from the components in the Dow-Jones index of industrial bonds than could be obtained from blue chip common shares in the Dow-Jones index of industrial common stocks.

Diversified common stock funds assume that the "best way to make your money grow" is by placing your bets on the growth of the economy. They keep most of their assets in common stocks at all times. Most emphasize long-term capital growth. Some also try to provide a fair dividend return.

Growth stock funds are the most popular and publicized common stock funds. Most buyers try for big capital gains and care little if at all for dividends. Many portfolio managers working the growth field even turn away from dividend-paying stocks. They argue that growth companies should be able to put earnings to work to produce more growth and that a corporation management that cannot invest its own earnings profitably will not perform dramatically. These funds invest heavily in "emerging companies" — those that have already shown, or give promise of showing, steadily rising earnings records that encourage large price-earnings ratios.

A 1971 study by Arthur Lipper and Company showed that such growth stock funds invested heavily in relatively unknown companies. More than 20 percent of the total shares outstanding (and in some cases more than 30 percent) of the following companies were held by funds: American Re-Insurance, Barnett Banks of Florida, Colwell Company, Informatics, International Foodservice Systems, Pier One Imports, Scope, Inc., Watkins-Johnson. In addition, of course, growth funds also had substantial positions in many better-known companies, such as Xerox, International Business Machines, and Avon.

Bond funds are investment trusts with the objective of lending money to industries, utilities, and states, cities, or other public bodies. Some such funds try to invest in issues that permit conversion into common stock; if the latter rises, they get not only reasonably assured income but also capital gains as their holdings rise with the common stock.

Municipal bond funds are currently popular. Their attraction lies in the fact that interest received on them is exempt from federal taxes and, usually, from taxes in the state of issuance. For example, the interest on New York City bonds is exempt from federal, state, and city income taxes. The higher your normal tax bracket, the more attractive these bonds become. If you reach a 50 percent tax level, you would need twice the return on taxable investments to equal the return you get from municipals.

Municipal bonds are of two types. "General obligation" bonds, issued by states and cities, are backed by the full taxing power of the issuing body and are considered second in safety only to the bonds of the federal government itself. "Revenue" bonds, issued to finance specific public projects such as toll highways and bridges, depend on revenues generated by those projects to pay the principal and interest. Hence they may be less secure than general obligation bonds. Defaults, while uncommon, have happened. (The West Virginia Turnpike and Calumet Skyway, for example, have had trouble producing the money to pay its bondholders.)

Unlike mutual funds that make portfolio changes as their

managers think fit, municipal bond funds often consist of fixed portfolios. The fund sponsor puts together a group of bonds; then the sponsor offers "units" of the total package to investors. Some groups may be of the highest grade (and therefore the lowest interest-payers); other groups may consist of more speculative but still of investment-quality bonds.

Funds for All Reasons

It is in the area of common stock funds that the greatest variety can be found. In addition to the majority of diversified funds, which choose their investments mainly from the broad range of stocks available on the national exchanges, hundreds of funds have been set up for special purposes. Or, as Wall Street cynics say, they have special sales gimmicks.

As its name suggests, the Over-the-Counter Securities Fund invests primarily in stocks not available on the exchanges. Other funds specialize in undersea products and services (Ocean Technology Fund, Oceanographic Fund) and in insurance stocks (Life Insurance Investors). Some funds concentrate on regions (Hawaii-Pacific Growth Fund, Israel American Diversified Fund, Japan Fund). The New Issues Fund seeks promising situations among companies going public for the first time.

The Rowe Price New Era Fund was set up specifically for shareholders who believe in the inevitability of inflation. "Long-term inflationary trends have made clear the importance of investing for capital growth," says its prospectus. "The management believes that investments in companies within certain industries and industry groups may offer more protection than others against erosion of capital due to decline in the purchasing power of the dollar." Organized in January, 1969, the fund has placed most of its assets in such stock groups as precious metals, energy sources, forest products, real estate, nonferrous metals, consumer and service groups, science, and technology.

Another registered investment company, operated by Quinby and Company in Rochester, New York, exists to accumulate shares for its shareholders in the common stock of American Telephone and Telegraph Company. Other Quinby funds exist to acquire shares variously in DuPont, Eastman Kodak, General Electric, General Motors, Standard Oil, and Xerox.

The advantage to the small investor is that the investor can buy a small number of shares in these funds without paying the high odd-lot and brokerage commissions incurred if the shares were bought directly.

Probably the most conservative of all funds is the Mutual Fund for Investing in Government Securities, Inc., which invests only in securities guaranteed by the U.S. government or its agencies. The word *conservative* has been used to emphasize the limited nature of the returns: while the investor in government securities will surely get back the number of dollars the government agrees to pay, and at the stipulated rate of interest, the investment fails to take into account the declining purchasing power of the dollar. Of course, government securities can be bought by anyone. Often, however, certain minimum denominations may be beyond the reach of the small investor. Therefore, the $250 minimum required to invest in this fund has a special appeal for the less-than-wealthy who seek what they regard as maximum security.

Some funds are admittedly high-risk operations — great when the risks pan out but miserable when they do not. One such enterprise, the Channing Venture Fund, managed by the Channing Company, was set up in October, 1970. The fund borrows from banks to put more money to work in the market, sells short (sells stock it does not own with hopes of buying it later at a lower price), and buys call options, which will enable it to buy the stock itself at a specified price at some later date. This is a "winner-take-all" technique because if the price of the stock goes up after the call option is purchased, a big profit is possible. But if the price of the stock does not rise, the option buyer loses all the money invested in the option. In addition, Channing buys into small, relatively unknown companies with a boom or bust potential. A 1971 survey of leading mutual funds by *FundScope* magazine revealed there are at least 15 funds that may sell short.

The *FundScope* study also revealed other techniques commonly employed by many funds in acquiring stock. Some 58 of the funds included in the survey may buy "on margin," that is, may borrow money in addition to the shareholders' investments in order to make purchases. Some 20 funds state in their prospectuses that they may use "puts and calls" — options to buy or sell stock at approximately today's prices but at a later date. Only 3 funds permitted trading in commodities and real estate, and only 2 said that they would ever seek to gain control of the companies in which they invested. Most funds did not invest in "restricted securities," those that cannot be sold to the public without being registered with the SEC. *FundScope* counted 8 funds with portfolios of more than 200 issues — one fund had holdings in 586 corporations — and found one with only 10 issues in its portfolio.

Among other types of funds in operation are the hedge funds. These relatively new additions to the mutual fund assortment aim to do exactly that: hedge. Some of their money is usually invested in stock on the long side, hoping for a profit as prices advance; some is invested in short positions in hopes of profit if prices drop. Running a successful hedge fund obviously calls for tremendous trading agility. Most hedge funds are partnerships. They sell their shares to a limited number of persons, do not register with the SEC, and do not offer shares to the public.

There are also specialty funds, though some are "special" in name only. Consider the Chemical Fund, with assets of some $600 million. Organized in the late 1930s, it has generally done somewhat better than average in both rising and falling markets. However, it is much less specialized than its name implies. It defines a "chemical company" as one whose business "is in the world of chemical science, research, and technology." With this umbrella over its portfolio it has invested heavily in corporations that are ordinarily not classified in the chemical field; these include corporations such as Polaroid, Xerox, and Eastman Kodak and drug manufacturers such as Johnson and Johnson and Merck. It also includes American Telephone and Telegraph Company (physical chemistry), Standard Oil of New Jersey (oil and gas), Avon Products (toiletries and cosmetics), and Procter and Gamble (consumer products). In truth, its portfolio looks little different from that of any other growth fund.

Funds with a Social Conscience

If you think business should try harder to solve social

problems of the day, even if it means lower profits, you can find several funds with the stated purpose of investing only in corporations that measure up to ecological and social standards. Such companies must, for examples, avoid pollution or actively train and employ members of minority groups. Among such funds are the Third Century Fund, a unit of the Dreyfus complex, and the Social Dimensions Fund, which seeks to "contribute to society beyond the satisfaction of basic material needs and the traditional goal of maximum profit, to the exclusion of all others."

One such fund, the First Spectrum Fund, intends, "as part of the regular security analysis," to "secure and analyze information on corporate responsibility . . . in respect to material matters involving the environment, civil rights, and the protection of consumers." The fund intends to avoid investments in any company with charges pending against it for violating pollution, civil rights, and consumer regulations. After investing in a "clean" company, if information later discloses the company "is in violation of statutory or administrative standards or . . . engaged in an environmental, civil rights, or consumer practice that is of questionable legality," the fund pledges (if it decides to retain such securities or any portion thereof) "to take whatever steps may be reasonable to attempt to correct such practice, including voting the fund's shares for shareholder proposals or changes in management designed to lead to the correction of the practice. . . ."

The prospectus further promises that "once invested in a company's stock, the fund, through its board of directors, intends to assert its voice as a stockholder to encourage the continuing formation of socially responsible corporate policy in areas where the fund believes the company's greatest competence can be applied."

First Spectrum also has approved a list of charitable or social nonprofit institutions from which shareholders may select those to which they wish to make contributions out of dividends. While shareholders need not participate in the plan, "the fund hopes that through the aggregate contributions of its shareholders the public good will be furthered."

Another fund with a social conscience, the Pax World Fund, of Portsmouth, New Hampshire, organized in August, 1971, eschews investments in a wide range of disapproved industries. As its name suggests, it is chary of companies engaged "in any degree" in manufacturing defense or weapon-related products. It "endeavors to make a contribution to world peace by investing in securities of companies whose business is essentially directed toward nonmilitary activities." It also tries to avoid investments in industries connected with the manufacture, sale, or promotion of liquor, tobacco, or gambling equipment. An open-end, no-load fund sponsored by the United Methodist church, the Pax Fund actively seeks investments in companies that conspicuously follow fair employment practices. With such criteria as guidelines for investment, the fund's president, Luther Tyson, admits that finding enough "100 percent pure" corporations in which to invest is difficult. Presented with such limited options, the fund has made some investments in corporations doing defense work, but only when defense contracts amounted to less than 5 percent of their total sales and the goods produced are not used in actual warfare.

In general, however, mutual funds are neutral with respect to social issues. As a massive study of institutional investors undertaken by the Securities and Exchange Commission noted:

> The existence of potential power on the part of institutions to influence corporate decisions by reason of their substantial shareholdings does not demonstrate that such influence is in fact exercised. . . . Such data as is available tend to show that institutions tend to vote with management on questions put to a shareholder vote and that if they lose confidence in management they tend to sell their holdings in a company rather than to attempt to control or influence management decisions. This conclusion appears attributable to two factors. First, institutions are inclined to believe that their responsibility is to make investment decisions rather than to attempt to influence management decisions. Second, while there are no statutory restrictions upon the right of institutions to attempt to influence management decisions, institutions tend to believe that an effort to do so would be inappropriate and would subject them to criticism.
>
> Institutions are more likely to take a definite position on questions which have a clear impact on their economic position and rights as shareholders. These include proposals to abolish preemptive rights, authorization of mergers, and authorization of

corporate acquisitions, particularly where such acquisition involves issuance of additional securities. In general, it can be concluded that even where institutions have the potential power to influence management decisions, they tend to be reluctant to exercise this power, particularly in an open and public way. While there are, no doubt, instances where institutions influence corporate decisions informally through personal consultations with management, reliable statistical evidence of the extent to which this occurs is not available.[1]

Funds for Special People

Many funds operate for a highly restricted clientele. The Common Fund for Nonprofit Organizations, started in 1971, manages the endowment funds of colleges and schools. The corporation was set up with the help of the Ford Foundation. McGeorge Bundy, the foundation's president, had previously criticized the investment policies of college endowment funds and commented, "Over the long run caution has cost our colleges much more than imprudence or excessive risk-taking." With the market value of the capital portfolios of American colleges and universities estimated at $12 to $14 billion, this cooperative fund could become one of the nation's largest.

The Washington Mutual Investors Fund is one of several funds that exist for trustees, guardians, executors, and administrators of estates who have been given the responsibility of investing other people's money — for example, the inheritance of a widow or minor children. Someone with such a fiduciary responsibility must be extremely careful where he or she invests. If the investment turns sour, the investor must be able to prove that no greater risk was taken than could be expected of any "prudent person." To help the prudent, special lists of stocks are prepared by state agents and by the Register of Wills and Clerks of the Probate Branch of the U.S. District Court for the District of Columbia. On the list are stocks of solidly established public utilities with gross revenues of at least $10 million a year or the likes of the Generals — Electric, Foods, Mills, and Motors — which take in at least $30 million a year and pass other earnings and assets tests. As might be expected, funds that invest in nothing but stocks on the "legal list" are not spectacular performers. Washington Mutual's asset increase per share has been a shade below the average of all mutual funds in bull markets, but it performs better than the average in bear markets.

In addition, there are funds that have been set up for pension fund managers and other institutional investors (Edie Special Institutional Fund, Institutional Investors Mutual Fund). There is a Government Employees Investment Fund, Lutheran Brotherhood Fund, NEA Mutual Fund for teachers, Nassau Physicians Guild Investing Company, and Teachers Association Mutual Fund of California. The Edie Fund selects securities in its portfolio to meet the special needs of tax-exempt charitable foundations, employee-benefit trusts, and pension and profit-sharing plans.

Set up solely for members of labor unions, the American Union Investment Fund has two major purposes: to help laboring people's capital grow "as protection against the declining purchasing power of the dollar" and to keep investments away from "any company that is antilabor or shows lack of interest in social and environmental problems." American Union Investment is a no-load fund with an investment management subsidiary of Bache and Company as its adviser, and Bache itself slated to receive most of its brokerage business. Its organizers have been encouraging union leaders to demand that contracts provide a certain hourly amount per worker to buy fund shares. They have also approached employers to set up payroll deduction plans by which employees could buy shares on a regular basis.

Many other funds have been created to answer the needs of "special people." For example, many cemetery owners who sell "perpetual care" plans (by which they guarantee to keep the grass cut on cemetery plots) are legally required to set aside a certain percentage of what they collect for that purpose. They may invest it in the Cemetery Care Investment Fund. Doctors, dentists, and other self-employed professionals have the PRO Fund with Standard and Poor's as its investment adviser.

Even Coca-Cola International Corporation operates a fund of its own, as do Pittsburgh Coke and Chemical Company, American-Hawaiian Steamship Company, Barber Oil Corporation, and Real Silk Hosiery Mills, among others.

Funds That Invest in Other Funds

As though investors do not give up enough responsibility by choosing a mutual fund manager to handle their money for them, some funds have been started with the idea, in effect, of choosing the fund managers for investors. Such funds, known as fund holding companies, invest wholly or largely in the shares of other investment companies. Their reasoning is that it takes expert knowledge to know which funds in which to invest.

Such funds lay additional costs — advisory fees, administrative expenses, sales loads, and brokerage fees — on investors. If you commit your money to a *fund of funds*, you not only bear your share of the advisory fees paid by each portfolio fund in which the holding company invests but you also bear a share of the advisory fee paid by the holding company to its adviser. When the fund holding company is a load fund, you must pay a sales charge to buy its shares as well as the sales charges that the holding company pays to acquire the shares of other funds. Moreover, you must pay twice for such services as stock transfer costs, dividend disbursements, custodial fees, and the cost of shareholder communications. The cost of such services is deducted from the income of the fund in which you invest directly, and it is also deducted from the income of the funds that your fund invests in.

Some funds of funds claim that they provide the added safety that comes with diversification. This claim, says the SEC, is largely illusory. The SEC states further:

> A mutual fund itself offers diversification in spreading its investments over a number of companies in different industries. A fund management will generally select the industries which it believes will perform best in the future and the best performing companies in those industries. Some funds invest in 30 or 40 companies, others in many more. Thus the diversification afforded by an ordinary mutual fund substantially reduces the risk of putting one's money in the one, two, or five stocks which an individual investor may buy.
>
> What does a fund of funds add to this diversification? Theoretically the risk is spread further since all the investor's "eggs" are not in one "basket" — one fund. Practically, however,

diversification upon diversification does not result in greater safety in proportion to the number of layers imposed on the original investment. Moreover, to the extent that greater diversification may be sought by spreading a single investment among several portfolio funds, the likelihood increases that the management of one portfolio fund will be buying for its portfolio the same securities the management of another will be selling, thereby subjecting the holding company's overall assets to brokerage fees for what are, in effect, wash transactions which achieve no investment purpose.

A fund holding company vehicle so duplicates and reduplicates the diversification achieved by the investment in a single fund that the expenses incurred defeat the investor's objective. Presumably a fund holding company investing in other fund holding companies [a fund of funds of funds] would provide even greater diversification, but the costs would obviously be out of proportion to whatever benefits the greater diversification may achieve.[2]

Thus has the SEC discredited the fund holding companies' claim that the diversification that they offer acts as an additional safety mechanism to protect their investments.

It also has argued against the desirability of a fund holding company on the ground that the proliferation of mutual funds, with varying records of performance, makes it difficult for the investor to choose the best-performing funds. Its reasoning goes like this.

A mutual fund investment offers professional management of a diversified portfolio. Once an investor elects this method of investing, he must select a professional investment manager (namely, a specific mutual fund). The investor alone must make this investment decision. If "professionals" are needed to choose among a group of professionals, professionals also must be needed to choose the professionals.

Furthermore, although the fund holding company aims to select the best-performing funds for acquisition (only a limited number of funds can qualify), the opportunities for investment must shrink in proportion to the growth of the top fund. Once the "best" funds are selected, only the "second best" remain. A fund holding company is sharply limited in the amounts it may invest in such funds and must spread its investments among a large number of them.

In its report on this question the SEC concluded:

> It is not at all clear that investors in a fund of funds profit from any more "informed choice" than is offered by management of an ordinary investment company. In order to reach a sound investment decision, management of a fund of funds must itself make much of the very same analysis and study of underlying securities necessary to operate any mutual fund and to this extent could operate their fund not as a holding company but as an ordinary mutual fund. Duplication of fees and expenses under such circumstances, in the absence of any clear benefits, can hardly be justified.[3]

One should not, however, underestimate the ingenuity of fund promoters. When no-load funds became popular, a fund of funds known as the Dern Fund itself charged the full sales commission — up to 8.5 percent — for its shares. For the relatively simple task of buying other funds this fund planned to pay its investment adviser an annual advisory fee of .75 percent of the net asset value — that is, 50 percent more than the customary fee. Still more remarkable, the initial contract with the investment adviser allowed the advisory fee to be increased to as much as 4 percent if the fund surpassed the Dow-Jones Industrial Average by a sufficient margin on the up side. On the other hand, the fee would not be reduced if the fund dropped more than the Dow-Jones Average. All of these fees, it should be noted, were paid by shareholders for the privilege of investing in mutual funds the shares of which could be bought without any sales commissions and with much lower advisory fees in the first place.*

The concept of a fund that invests in other funds has been badly clouded by the "Cornfeld caper," involving the rise and subsequent fall of Bernard Cornfeld's mutual fund empire, the Investors Overseas Services. How Bernie Cornfeld, a bright lad

---

*In 1970 the Investment Company Act of 1940 was amended to prevent just such escalation of charges. The Dern Fund was required to reduce its sales charge to a maximum of 1.5 percent upon the purchase of shares costing less than $10,000. Another amendment prohibited the advisory fee that increased when the fund did well but did not decrease when the fund did poorly.

from Brooklyn, went to Paris in 1955 and began selling mutual funds is much too complex to be recounted here. In brief, however, Cornfeld discovered the truth (which most fund salespeople soon learn) that customers can be persuaded to invest thousands of dollars without the vaguest idea of what they are buying. To free himself from the hampering restrictions imposed upon investment companies based in the United States, Cornfeld set up — among several "offshore" funds — a Fund of Funds, which would invest in other mutual funds. Cornfeld was undeniably a supersalesman with the ability to inspire others to supersales efforts. But the talents required to create a huge fund are not the same ones needed to operate it successfully for the shareholders.

The Fund of Funds was based on the assumption, of course, that professional managers can do a better job at selecting outstanding funds than can the ordinary individual. Investors in this fund could have done better on their own. From the time of its launching, in 1962, until December 31, 1969, the net asset value of the Fund of Funds grew by 127.2 percent — a substantial increase but markedly worse than the growth of the average American fund during the same period. As a result of some incredibly poor investments as well as the bear market of 1970, the net asset value of each share in the Fund of Funds plummeted to $7.44 — less than two-thirds of the price per share that the original investors paid eight years before.

Funds That Aren't Mutual

There are other kinds of investment companies besides mutual funds. Like mutual funds, they are managed by professionals for shareholders, but they differ from mutual funds in one or more important aspects.

Such funds include the following.

Closed-end investment companies may operate in much the same way as mutual funds, but they do not continuously sell shares to the public in order to obtain new capital. Mutual funds, on the other hand, are open-end. They are ready and willing, except under extraordinary circumstances, to sell new shares or redeem old ones.

An investor in a closed-end company cannot redeem shares

at the office of the issuing company. The investor must find someone to sell to — the usual procedure followed if an investor wishes to sell shares in General Motors, for example. The price at which closed-end shares sell depends, therefore, upon what a buyer will pay. This in turn may have no close relationship to the actual asset value per share. In general, shares of closed-end companies sell at substantial discounts (considerably less than the actual assets per share) in bear markets. During bull markets the discount may be greatly narrowed, and the shares may even sell at a premium (more than the assets are actually worth).

In contrast, the price of shares in mutual funds theoretically is closely pegged to what would be received were the underlying assets sold and the cash distributed to the shareholders. As we shall see, the stated asset value per share may be incredibly wide of the true mark. Nevertheless, so long as the mutual fund remains fully operational, the shareholder can be confident of obtaining this stated value whenever he sells his holdings.

One reason closed-end companies often sell at a discount is that they usually make no effort to promote continued stockholder interest in their shares. They do not use salespeople and generally do not advertise. One exception is the Lehman Company, a diversified investment company, which ran advertisements in the fall of 1971 stating: "Shares may now be purchased at less than net asset value through your New York Stock Exchange broker."

Non-diversified investment companies constitute, in effect, the difference between closed- and open-end funds. There is also a functional difference between investment companies based upon their classifications as *diversified* or *nondiversified*.

According to the Investment Company Act of 1940 a diversified company invests (with respect to 75 percent of its total assets) not more than 5 percent of its total assets in the securities of any company and not more than 10 percent in securities representing the outstanding voting securities of any company.

Most open-end mutual funds are diversified because this classification carries important tax benefits. For example, diversified funds pay no income tax if they distribute at least 90 percent of their ordinary income to their shareholders in the form of dividends. (The shareholders, of course, must pay a tax on dividends received.) Moreover, diversified funds pay no direct tax on net long-term capital gains. They may pass the gains on to shareholders, who then pay the tax, often at a lower rate than the corporation would have to pay. Or they may hold the gains, adding to the asset value per share, and pay the tax for the shareholders. (If this tax is greater than the shareholder would have to pay, the latter may file for a refund.) As a result of the 1940 Act, therefore, few diversified investment companies pay a federal corporate income tax. Although not required to do so, most distribute all or substantially all of their net long-term capital gains to their shareholders.

Nondiversified funds, according to the Investment Company Act of 1940, refer to investment trusts that have over-concentrated their assets in a few holdings and consequently cannot satisfy the prerequisites for diversification. Included in this category are some small business investment companies and other venture capital companies that invest in small firms with expected growth potential. One such investment company is the Narragansett Capital Corporation, a company with 20-plus investments but more than half of its assets invested in only 4 of them.

Dual-purpose funds have two purposes, as their name implies. They offer income shares for the investor primarily interested in security in the form of consistent dividends and capital shares for the investor more concerned about long-term increases in the value of the investment. These funds are organized so that income shareholders receive the dividends and interest not only from their own shares but also from the shares held by the capital shareholders. After a stipulated period their shares are redeemed at a specified price whether or not anything remains to distribute to its capital shareholders. On the other hand, the capital shareholders benefit from the appreciation in value of both kinds of shares.

Dual-purpose funds are closed-end. After issuance their shares are only worth what others will pay for them. Since their introduction, in the 1960s, shares in these funds have generally sold at prices below the value of their underlying assets.

Real estate investment trusts are similar to mutual funds, but they invest in real estate instead of stocks. They are required to invest 75 percent or more of their gross assets in real estate loans, property, cash, and government securities and must derive 75 percent or more of their gross income from real estate transactions. Upon distribution of at least 90 percent of their ordinary income to shareholders they too are exempt from corporate income and capital gains taxes.

The Fund Explosion: Boon or Bane for Investors?

According to the mutual fund industry, the wide variety of investment companies assures any investor of finding precisely the kind of management company and portfolio that is desired.

This is true if enough investment counselors are available to provide the investor with the kind of up-to-date, disinterested information required in order to make a selection from among the numerous funds in operation. Unfortunately, such counselors are in extremely short supply, and most fund salespeople for one reason or another make a rudimentary selection for their customers. Also, since they sell shares in a rather limited number of funds (rarely more than a dozen), it is one of these that their customer will be sold.

In fact, the multiplication of investment companies — from the archconservative to the dice-rolling speculative — sharply increases the chances that the individual investor will be offered and, if possible, sold a fund that is totally unsuitable. Instead of making it easier for the average person to participate in the market and take a place among the "shareholders in America," the growth of both the number and the scope of funds has made the task much more difficult and perilous.

3

How Well Do Funds Perform?

Iт is no secret, among brokers at least, that as a group, investment companies hardly perform as well as their salespeople represent. In *Security Analysis*, the Bible of professional analysts, Graham, Dodd, and Cottle observed that investment trusts as a whole "have been unable to equal the performance of a comprehensive stock market index."[1] Moreover, every objective study of funds has reached a similar conclusion. For example, a detailed study for the period 1927-1935 by staff members of the Securities and Exchange Commission concluded with considerable assurance: "The entire group of management investment companies proper failed to perform better than an index of leading common stocks and probably performed somewhat worse than the index over the 1927-1935 period."

Graham, Dodd, and Cottle also measured the 1951-1960 performance record of 58 investment companies against the results achieved by Standard and Poor's Composite Index of

27

500 common stocks. The results agreed with earlier findings: only 3 investment companies exceeded the composite performance. While the 500 representative stocks in Standard and Poor's list gained 322 percent over the 10-year period, the investment companies had a mean gain of only 221 percent. The researchers drily commented: "These results do not appear as satisfactory as they should be."[2]

A highly publicized study under the direction of Professor Irwin Friend, of the Wharton School of Finance (of the University of Pennsylvania), compared performances of funds with common stock indexes for several periods in the 1950s. It says in part:

> Standard and Poor's Composite Common Stock Index was definitely superior to the average performance of the funds, but the disparity can be explained by the portfolio structure of the funds, i.e., the division of their portfolios among common stocks, preferred stocks, corporate bonds, government securities, and other assets. When adjustments are made for the composition, the average performance by the funds did not differ appreciably from what would have been achieved by an unmanaged portfolio with the same division among asset types.[3]

The Wharton researchers concluded that an unmanaged portfolio (one with stocks randomly selected) could achieve results as favorable as those obtained by funds in general. In addition, the study found that half the professional managers achieved results that were markedly worse than the individual investor could have achieved by selecting stocks at random. (Half the portfolio managers performed better, of course.)

Later an updated study of fund performance by Professor Friend and two other professors of finance at the University of Pennsylvania, Marshal E. Blume and Jean Crockett, was made under the auspices of the Twentieth Century Fund.

Their analysis included all funds for which they could obtain reliable monthly price and dividend data and covered the periods from January, 1960, through June, 1968; January, 1960, through March, 1964; and April, 1964, through June, 1968. Almost all mutual funds were included except very small ones and those formed after April, 1964. The funds included in the study held 89 percent of the estimated total assets of all funds as of December 31, 1967.

Friend, Blume, and Crockett found that overall annual rates of return on investment (reflecting capital gains and dividends) for the funds studied averaged 10.7 percent for the period of January, 1960, through June, 1968, 9.0 percent for the period from January, 1960, through March, 1964, and 12.8 percent for the period from April, 1964, through June, 1968. They compared these rates with corresponding rates of return for all common stocks listed on the New York Stock Exchange. They made two comparisons: one with a portfolio in which equal investments were made in each stock listed on the Exchange and the other with a portfolio in which investments were weighted to conform to the value of the outstanding stock in each listed company. They found that investments in the first portfolio would have yielded annual rates of return of 12.4 percent, 7.0 percent, and 17.8 percent, respectively, for the three periods covered. The proportional (weighted) investment would have produced annual rates of 9.9, 9.9, and 9.8 percent for the respective periods.

The results were significant: equally weighted or unweighted investment in NYSE stocks would have resulted in a higher rate of return than that achieved by mutual funds in the 1960–1968 period as a whole (a lower rate in the first half of that period and a much higher rate in the second half). In contrast, proportionately weighted investment in NYSE stocks would have resulted in a lower rate of return in the period as a whole — a higher rate in the first half and a lower rate in the second half. Their conclusion: "It appears from these results that random portfolios of New York Stock Exchange stocks with equal investment in each stock performed on the average better over the period than did mutual funds of the same risk class."[4]

Arthur Lipper and Company, a New York Stock Exchange firm specializing in investment company research, gives a weekly report on the performance of each mutual fund vis-à-vis other funds and the Dow-Jones and Standard and Poor's averages. The Lipper report shows that funds as a group tend to outperform the stock averages in rising markets, but they lose more in falling markets.

For example, in 1968, a year marked by an early downturn and then a sharp run-up leading to a bull market climax, the Dow-Jones Industrial Average increased 4.3 percent; Standard and Poor's index of 500 stocks increased 7.66 percent; and the New York Stock Exchange composite index increased 9.4 percent. A computation of 307 funds by Lipper showed that they experienced an average increase of 18.25 percent. Two hundred and eighty-five did better than the Dow average; 237 also outdistanced the NYSE index. Indeed, by this measurement, fund performance was impressive.

However, in that year a large number of funds invested in little-known companies listed on the American Stock Exchange. The ASE index of stocks traded on that exchange showed a more spectacular gain, 33.44 percent. Most of the best performers were small funds with investments in relatively small companies. The Neuwirth Fund (assets: $63 million) gained 90 percent for first place honors, and the Gibraltar Growth Fund (assets: $25 million) was second, with an increase of 72.7 percent. Poorest performers that year were some of the largest and best-known funds. Gerald Tsai's highly publicized Manhattan Fund was down 6.9 percent. The 70 funds that failed to equal the NYSE average held $21 million (43 percent) of the total assets under fund management. Conclusion: the industry's achievement for the year was less than brilliant.

Figures for 1969 were even less inspiring. The average mutual fund performed better than the Dow-Jones and ASE indexes but worse than the Standard and Poor's and NYSE composite indexes (funds, a minus 14.43 percentage; ASE, minus 19.71; Dow-Jones, minus 15.19; NYSE, minus 12.51 percent; Standard and Poor's, minus 11.36 percent). Of 376 funds followed by Lipper only 19 gained in net assets for the year. (Templeton Growth Fund led the list with a gain of 19.38 percent; the Canadian and International Fund, Ltd., managed by Loomis-Sayles, was second, with a gain of 11.04 percent.) Losses for many went beyond 25 percent, and in a dozen cases the loss exceeded 35 percent.

In the 1970 seesaw market (most prices sharply down in the first half and sharply up in the second) the funds demonstrated that they fluctuate with the averages. It is hard for them to gain while the averages are falling. For the year, 463 funds of all types had a decline of 9.41 percent versus gains of 4.82 percent for the Dow-Jones Average and .1 percent for the Standard and Poor's Index. Growth funds were even more volatile: in 1970 they declined 15.97 percent. The average fund did worse than all the major indexes except the ASE index, which itself declined 13.40 percent.

Not all funds performed that poorly. Indeed, one small growth income mutual fund took first place in performance, with a gain of 18 percent. Several others came close to that, and more than 100 funds out of 467 finished on the plus side in 1970 despite the severe slump of the first five months.

On the other hand, one fund decreased 56 percent in value in the twelve-month period, and several were almost as bad. More than 120 funds recorded losses ranging from 20 to 56 percent despite the major price recovery of the last half of 1970. This was much worse than any average.

"That's a simply horrible performance," wrote economist Sylvia Porter, "and hardly an ad for the mutual fund industry."[5]

In 1971 the industry's performance was more impressive. Whereas the average of 526 funds showed a gain of 18.10 percent for the year, a gain of only 6.11 percent was recorded for the Dow-Jones Industrials, 10.79 percent for Standard and Poor's 500, 12.34 percent for the NYSE composite, and 12.48 percent for the ASE index.

Other Research Revelations

Other measurements have been made to determine how well fund portfolio managers really perform. SEC investigators compared fund investment results with those achieved from investments in the common stocks that small investors favored in the period 1957-1965. *Odd-lotters* are those who buy and sell in quantities lower than the unit (usually 100 shares) traded on the Exchange. In the period studied the stocks that small investors traded most actively included such blue chips as American Telephone and Telegraph, U.S. Steel, Chrysler Corporation, General Motors, and Standard Oil Company.

"Odd-lotters are always wrong," claim Wall Street experts. On the other hand, the investigators found that while "investments in mutual funds, with their diversified portfolios of securities, present less risk to investors than alternative investments in individual securities," in most cases "a majority of the investments in the stocks favored by odd-lot investors would have yielded higher proceeds than the median mutual fund investment." They observed that the one factor contributing to the poorer performance of mutual funds as compared to odd-lot investors is that mutual fund investors are initially saddled with higher costs. The report stated:

> The most significant factor is the high initial cost of investment (in mutual funds). Where the typical investor in common stocks receives about $980 worth of stock for a $1,000 investment, the typical mutual fund investor received only $915 worth of fund shares. A greater percentage of investments in common stocks liquidated a few years after their purchase had higher proceeds than the median mutual funds, while a lesser percentage of the common stock investments held for longer periods of time had higher proceeds. This tends to support the assumption that the initial costs are a significant cause of the relatively lower fund proceeds.[6]

One of the most comprehensive studies of mutual funds ever made showed that random choice — the equivalent to throwing a dart at a stock market listing — had about as successful a record as mutual funds. In a project supported by the brokerage firm of Merrill Lynch, Pierce, Fenner and Smith, Professors Lawrence Fisher and James H. Lorie, of the University of Chicago, ran millions of figures through a computer and discovered that anyone who invested equal amounts in every common stock listed on the New York Exchange at any time from January, 1926, until December, 1964, and held the stock until the 1964 date would have gained at least 8.2 percent a year, compounded annually with the dividends reinvested. Had you bought the stocks in January, 1926, you would have made 9.3 percent a year, compounded. Had you bought them at any time since 1931 and held them until 1964, you would have made at least 12.4 percent a year. In view of these results Professor Lorie concluded, "The evidence is accumulating that it is very hard for portfolio managers to surpass the return on random selection. It's no secret that mutual funds on the average do about as well as the market — so why pay the 8 percent charge?" [7]

One measurement of the competence of fund managers is what happens to the stocks that they buy or sell. Because they claim to possess superior wisdom, the stocks they buy on balance should rise; stocks they sell should fall. Such a test of fund buying and selling activity for the first quarter of 1971 (ending on March 31) was made by *Forbes* magazine. It measured the prices (as of June, 1971) of the 25 listed stocks most heavily bought and the 25 most heavily sold by the funds. The purchase and sale price for the first quarter was the weighted average price of total transactions of the individual stocks. The result: among the shares bought on balance 18 had risen by June 30 and 7 had declined; among the stocks sold on balance 17 had risen, and 8 had declined. Of the 50 stocks included in the test the one that rose most during this period was Sony, of which the funds had dumped 90,470 shares, with a price appreciation of 52.3 percent. The stock that experienced the greatest decline was Allis Chalmers, of which the funds had bought 1,502,000 shares on balance; it dropped 24.4 percent. Some other stocks discarded by the funds included Kresge, which experienced a subsequent price rise of 32.9 percent; Upjohn, up 28.8 percent; Texas Instruments, up 27.4 percent; and Xerox, up 22 percent. Of the 16 stocks sold by the funds on balance 11 rose more than 10 percent.

The *Forbes* study found that the stocks that were sold most heavily performed approximately as well as the stocks that were bought most heavily. Whether results over a longer term would throw a more favorable light on the funds' judgment is unknown. But, the magazine commented, "Taking the fund industry as a whole, the immediate effects of its portfolio shifting were hardly brilliant."[8]

Truly "professional" management of growth funds would invest in young though obscure companies that experience faster-than-average growth. Friend, Blume, and Crockett tested the professionals' ability to achieve this standard, and they analyzed the relationship between stocks bought and later earnings on these issues. After extensive computations they concluded: "Mutual funds do not do particularly well or poorly in directing capital into profitable stock investments. . . . The funds seem just as likely to invest in a NYSE stock which proves to be overvalued in the light of its later earnings as in an undervalued issue. In fact, funds appear to have bought more stock that in the long run turned out to be overvalued than stock that turned out to be undervalued."[9]

The Friend-Blume-Crockett team could find no evidence that funds with higher sales charges, management costs, or trading expenses achieved better results for their shareholders than funds operating at minimum cost. They suggested:

> Because no clear payoff results from higher management and trading expenses, a new type of mutual fund with minimal management and trading may be desirable. Such a fund would resemble the fixed or semifixed trusts of former years. These trusts deliberately duplicated the performance of all NYSE stocks or of some other broad range of investments.
>
> This new kind of fund would provide, at minimal cost, the risk diversification which seems to be the most important continuing service rendered by today's mutual funds. The larger this fund might be, the smaller would be the relative management expenses, and the easier it would be to duplicate the performance of the entire market. Such large funds would become sufficiently well known to the investing public for their shares to be sold at commission rates appreciably lower than the sales loads now charged by mutual funds.[10]

Is Performance the Real Test?

Mutual fund representatives do not appreciate the comparison of investment procedures with the numbers game. "I am getting sick and tired of reading about the sorry performance of mutual funds," Harold Eichhorn, of the executive committee of the National Fund Managers Association, fumed in a letter to the *New York Times* in 1970. He continued:

> It is true that asset values are down, but it is also true that we have had one of the most severe market collapses since 1929. The disastrous performance of some funds was only a commentary on the public's desire for spectacular profits. Those who stayed with

the tried and true managements such as Fidelity, Massachusetts Investors, Chemical and Wellington — while a little battered — have done much better than the market.

It is also a sad commentary when Dr. Irwin Friend discovers that an investment in every stock in the market would have been equal or a little better than the average performance of all funds together in the 1960s. Can you tell me who could have bought every stock on the board? Mutual funds are living, performing corporate entities managed by human beings and not just a set of statistics. Looking at the other side of the coin, does anyone have the least conception of the types of stock the average investor bought throughout the 1960s? Why doesn't Professor Friend make a study of portfolios of the average stock buyers and results thereof? The findings would be really eye-opening and would make even the worst of mutual funds smell like a rose. Why doesn't the SEC foster such a study instead of worrying about sales charges and management fees of the funds? These costs would then stand out as a modicum of cheapness as compared to the underwriting fees and churning commissions paid by the individual stock buyers during this period.[11]

It is certainly true that many small investors, advised by brokers or making investment decisions on their own, regularly take a beating in the market. This is to be expected. "Playing the market" is not a game for children. But the little investors do not put themselves forward as professionals with special expertise. To cite the analogy that fund salespeople like to employ, the individual who tries to remove his own appendix is expected to botch the job. But to carry the analogy further, when a surgeon does no better, it is a matter of professional malfeasance.

In general, though the statistics have not always been favorable, funds have not rejected the performance concept. Many have embraced it heartily. One example of their performance mania is illustrated by the sharp rise in the turnover of their common stock holdings — a reflection of their desire to take advantage of every swing in the market.

In 1953 funds turned over only 13.1 percent of their total shares. They were content to buy into companies because they saw prospects for long-term gains and were not swayed by temporary fluctuations. In the mid-sixties, however, it became a new ball game, and the "now" generation won out: fund managers had to outperform their competitors week by week. In contrast with 1955, when funds on the average turned over only one-sixth of their holdings, 20 percent of the shares held by funds were moved out of their strong boxes in 1965. By 1969 the turnover rate had jumped to 50 percent; of every two shares in the boxes on the first of the year, one had been sold by the year's end.

Of course, in this trend mutual funds were not alone. Other institutions (banks, pension funds, insurance companies, etc.) also have been turning over their stock faster than ever before. (The turnover ratio of life insurance companies nearly doubled between 1966 and 1969, as did that of private pension funds, while the turnover ratio of fire and casualty companies tripled. Yet the ratios for these groups remained well below those for open-end investment companies.) Such stock switching by institutional investors increased the overall turnover ratio on the New York Stock Exchange from 15 percent in 1965 to 33 percent in 1969.[12]

Most of the growth that the securities industry experienced in the sixties was due to the increased activity of institutional investors. Institutional trading volume on the New York Stock Exchange increased by 548 percent during the decade, as compared with a 133 percent increase in business transacted by individuals. Whereas in 1959 institutional trading made up only a quarter of the public volume, in 1969 it was half of the total volume and still growing fast. During this decade the average size of mutual fund orders increased from 550 to 3,726 shares.[13]

"The growth in institutional trading," an SEC study reported, "had a significant effect on the profitability of New York Stock Exchange member firms." Retail firms — those dealing mainly with individuals with an average commission per transaction of less than $50 — have been much less profitable in recent years than have firms dealing primarily with institutions. Nineteen sixty-eight median pretax profits for all retail firms was $671,000. For institutional firms it was $2.4 million — almost four times as much. Although institutional firms represent only 13 percent of all NYSE member firms, they accounted for

52 percent of the firms earning $5 million and over. Fewer than 10 percent of the institutional firms (but 70 percent of the retail firms) had pretax profits under $1 million.

The SEC study noted:

> These disparities in pretax profits were due almost entirely to differences in the profitability of the security commission business. Although the retail firms as a group received two-thirds of all gross security commission income, only one-third of the pretax profits on this business. On the other hand, whereas institutional firms as a group received only 14 percent of all security commission income, they accounted for 39 percent of the pretax profits of all firms. Pretax profit margins on the security commission business itself were 5 percent for retail firms, as compared to 27 percent for institutional firms.

Despite their sharing of commission with retail firms, institutional firms achieved higher profit margins in 1968. For the most part, this reflected the current commission rate schedule, which did not recognize economies of scale. According to a study for the NYSE, the average cost of handling a 1,000- , a 10,000- , and a 100,000-share order of a $40 stock was, respectively, 6, 42, and 377 times the 100-share commission. Yet the commission fee charged in 1968 was, respectively, 10, 100, and 1,000 times the 100-share commission.[14] Now, however, mutual funds may negotiate brokers' fees on large trades. Nevertheless, brokers still find a few large trades substantially more profitable than a few thousand small ones.

The pressure on portfolio managers to make their fund a top performer sometimes reaches intense levels. George J. W. Goodman, editor of *Institutional Investor*, quotes one fund executive:

> It's as bitterly competitive as a pro-football league with a tight race. Every day we have our salesmen calling up, saying give us a record to sell, give us performance. Every day, we check the gain or loss of our portfolio against our competitors. When one of my competitors outperforms me, I check: How did he do it? Was his timing better catching the airlines? Why did he sell the textiles before we did, was his information better? It's a business that's going to burn up people pretty rapidly, because the guys who are

good in one kind of market aren't good in the next, and the pressure is there all the time, in every kind of market. It's going to be as much of a pressure business as Madison Avenue.[15]

According to Goodman, the emphasis on timing has induced many performance funds to operate a "war room." The charts that cover the walls have a strange resemblance to those found at a Strategic Air Command base. "In them, the chartists hunch over the boards, tracking the pattern and volume of stock movements, trying to find the proper points at which to buy and sell," stated Goodman.[16]

"Performance" funds — those trying to maximize weekly or monthly asset gains — almost by nature have short-term objectives. They attempt to predict "intermediate" swings of a few months. But many fund managers assert the impossibility of profiting from market trend predictions. In its semiannual report for the period ending in June, 1971, the management of the T. Rowe Price Growth Stock Fund expressed this viewpoint:

> We have never pretended to have much expertise in fore-casting the future course of the stock market. However, after monitoring the results of many different market technicians and reviewing innumerable theories as to how to predict the stock market, we do not believe that anyone else can consistently do this either. The market seems to have an uncanny knack for confounding the experts — particularly at important turning points.

Rather than devoting a lot of time to trying to guess which direction the market may go, a fund such as the T. Rowe Price Growth Stock Fund concentrates its efforts on trying to determine what a share in a growth company is worth. T. Rowe Price Growth states:

> This is not a simple determination. Our research analysts spend many days and weeks in the field each year interviewing top management of the companies in your portfolio, as well as talking to competitors and others. In addition, we employ the services of outside consultants such as Arthur D. Little, Inc. and Stanford Research Institute. The industries in which portfolio

companies operate are continually monitored to ensure that they remain fertile areas for growth of earnings. Corporate objectives and strategies are carefully analyzed to determine how realistic they are in the competitive and economic environment we visualize. A company's new product program, marketing efforts, labor developments, and changes in government regulation are among the things we watch carefully. Profitability, return on capital, and cash resources are analyzed to determine whether a company can adequately finance its anticipated growth . . . .

After making the above evaluations we then establish buying or selling programs for individual securities. A declining stock market, of course, helps to expedite our buying programs, and a rising market enables us to sell securities at levels in excess of what we think they are worth.

It can be seen that we are frequently working against prevailing stock market trends. Our judgment will not always be right. But we believe our procedure of letting reserves build up as individual stocks become overvalued and then putting our buying reserves to work when their prices decline to levels which we think they are worth is a far more logical and reliable procedure than trying to guess short-term market swings.

While many fund managers operate along these same lines ("Choose good stocks when the price is right"), others dismiss this approach as old-fashioned. Critics complain that this type of investment program generally lacks excitement — a quality that the new breed of fund managers increasingly stress.

Some funds implicitly admit they should not be expected to do better than the standard stock averages. They make such an admission by asking for incentive payments — in some cases as much as 6 percent — whenever their portfolios demonstrate greater appreciation than that reflected by the broad stock averages.

Why Can't Funds Do Better?

Despite their professional expertise, contacts with public corporations and managements and the great deal of time and energy expended in search of outstanding stocks, fund managers as a group fail to outperform the market in any decisive way. What factors explain this failure, which baffles even the experts?

Friend, Blume, and Crockett suggested the following partial answers:

> A sizable fund may have a hundred securities in its portfolio to obtain the very considerable benefits of diversification. Since there will be some differences of opinion as well as investment policy among fund managers, it would not be surprising to find as many as five hundred stocks extensively held in the combined portfolios of a hundred or more mutual funds. For obvious reasons the funds will tend to invest principally in the larger stocks among the New York Stock Exchange issues. These 500 issues might be expected to largely duplicate the performance of stock outstanding on the Big Board, since they may account for fully 90 percent of the value of such stock. Moreover, there is a very strong intercorrelation among the annual rates of return for different stocks, with the return on most individual stocks over longer periods tending to concentrate around the average return in the market as a whole. Finally, the inability of the larger funds to invest as much in the smaller and what, at least retrospectively, have turned out to be the more promising investments as they have in others also appears to have harmed their performance results.[17]

A comprehensive study of the investment policies of large funds shows them especially vulnerable to elephantiasis: their nature virtually requires them to buy and sell *large* blocks of securities. Although no law keeps them from investing in hundreds, or even thousands, of securities, their managers generally limit portfolio holdings to a far smaller number, which they think they can analyze and follow more effectively. Consequently, the favorite stocks in the mammoth funds invariably are those of corporations with tens or hundreds of millions of shares outstanding, namely, International Business Machines, General Motors, Xerox, and other behemoths.

Managers of large funds seldom consider the thousands of companies the shares of which are sold over-the-counter; so few shares of such firms are outstanding that an order for even a few thousand could cause the price to jump or plummet. Some funds set minimums on the amounts they will invest in one company. For example, one large fund tries to avoid investing less than $3 million in a single security.

Even when confining themselves to the country's 500 largest corporations, managers of the big funds often have trouble acquiring the number of shares they want at an attractive price. For example, a fund with assets of $500 million that wants to invest only 1 percent of its assets in a company on the Big Board at a price of 40 must buy 125,000 shares. Unless it can find a big-block seller among the other institutions, it will be forced to wait months to pick up that quantity either by buying smaller blocks when they are offered or "nibbling" in the open market. Buying more shares over a short period would upset the price.

Of equal significance was the SEC finding that large funds also encounter serious problems in disposing of large blocks of securities. Although funds seldom hold as much as 5 percent or more of a company's outstanding stock, even 1 or 2 percent frequently amounts to as much as 25 percent of the annual trading volume in the stock:

> Portfolio holdings of this size severely affect a fund's mobility by making it difficult, if not impossible, to react promptly to shifts in market trends. The disposition of such large blocks through the exchange or over-the-counter market at the time of the investment decision is sometimes impossible, and a fund's inability to react promptly to investment decisions sometimes causes it to "miss the market." In declining markets this lack of mobility can result in substantial losses or reductions in possible gains. An adviser to one of the largest funds spotted unfavorable factors affecting one of their portfolio securities. A decision to sell their holdings of almost 220,000 shares was made at a time when the market was $57 a share. However, before much of their selling program could be effected, the market price dropped to the mid-forties. In rising markets a fund's inability to promptly dispose of securities in response to investment decisions seriously affects its ability to switch in more promising securities.
>
> Because of the difficulties of disposing of large blocks of securities through normal market channels, funds are relying to an increasing extent on secondary distribution techniques which are more costly than normal market channels. However, in declining markets or where buying interest in a particular security is scant, a fund is sometimes unable to dispose of a large block of securities even through a secondary distribution. Under such

circumstances, the fund can either retain the security in the hope that market conditions will improve or dispose of it gradually through the regular exchange markets, the third market, and perhaps a secondary distribution of a portion of the block. Such a gradual disposition may take considerable time and often results in the fund realizing substantially less for the securities than if it had been able to dispose of the entire block promptly. In any event, it makes difficult the prompt execution of investment decisions and the reinvestment of funds.[18]

Sometimes large funds cannot acquire quantities of a security in order sufficiently to meet their analysts' recommendation. The adviser to one large fund recommended a purchase of 490,000 shares of a company. Six months later, the fund had bought only 35 percent of the shares sought. Another fund determined to purchase 50,000 shares of a company; two and a half years later orders for 10,700 shares had not been filled.

These problems may be compounded when a fund manager decides to buy a particular security for more than one fund within the complex. One fund manager authorized the purchase of almost 443,000 shares of one company for two funds under his management. Six months later less than 50 percent of the purchase order of one fund and only 10 percent of the purchase order of the other fund had been filled. The price per share increased from $40 to $48 in the interim.[19]

Funds seeking to buy or sell large blocks are often victimized by the specialists on the New York, American, and other national exchanges the privileged position of which enables them to learn about future transactions. In theory, these specialists stabilize the market by bringing buyers and sellers together. But when an excess of either buyers or sellers occurs, the specialists buy or sell for their own accounts. Since they keep the book of orders that have been placed to buy below or sell above the present price, they possess privileged information about a stock's underlying strength or weakness. It is not uncommon for them to take advantage of this information for their own profit. When the specialists know of, for example, major buying by an institutional investor such as a fund, the fund's position is made precarious at best.

An executive of the enormous Investors Diversified Services Fund recently placed an order to buy 700 shares of a $254 stock with a broker. As he watched the tape, the sale's price declined from $254 to $252. An investigation later revealed that the specialist had sold the stock which he did not own, to IDS at $254, then quickly bought it at $252 from other sellers to cover his short position. He made a quick profit of $1,400 — at the fund's expense.

On another occasion IDS wanted to buy a block of 250,000 shares traded on the New York Stock Exchange at approximately $80 a share. Since the specialist said he could not supply the stock at that price, through a broker IDS found a holder of that number of shares willing to sell at that price. However, according to the rules, a trade would have to be made on the Exchange through the specialist. Suddenly the panic-stricken broker called the IDS trader. Instead of serving as a conduit, the specialist wanted to buy 50,000 shares from the broker for his own account. Ostensibly he intended to grab those shares at $80 and resell them to IDS at a substantial profit for himself. In this case the specialist was thwarted because the buyer and seller took their transaction to the Midwest Stock Exchange.[20]

Of course, specialists have no favorites: they will victimize individuals just as readily as they will funds. The fact that funds deal in large blocks, however, makes them particularly attractive. The ultimate victims, naturally, are the fund's shareholders.

When he was chairman of the SEC, Manuel E. Cohen often expressed the view that the buyer of fund shares does not get the performance deserved because so much of the money is eaten away by commission fees (as much as 9 percent) paid to acquire the shares. According to Cohen, the superior performance of the average unmanaged portfolio is attributable to several factors. Cohen has stated:

> . . . the main reason is the high costs associated with a mutual fund investment, including the initial sales load, the annual advisory fees, and the recurring brokerage costs associated with the relatively high portfolio turnover rates of mutual funds.
> Studies by the Commission's staff, comparing mutual fund performance with the performance of individual stocks, various groups of stocks, and other measures of stock market performance,

also show that the high cost of a mutual fund investment tends to place the mutual fund investor at a disadvantage. These are the individual stocks that, in fact, have attracted the widespread interest of the smaller investor. For example, in one series of studies the Commission's staff compared the results of $1,000 investments in mutual fund shares made at the beginning of 1950, 1955, and 1960 and held for various periods of time with results from investing the same amount in those common stocks most favored by odd-lot investors. The stocks included such favorites as General Motors Corp., United States Steel Corp., American Telephone and Telegraph Co., and Standard Oil Co. of New Jersey. During most of these periods the majority of the investments in the most favored common stocks did better than the median mutual fund investment.

It is undeniable that, generally, investments in mutual funds, with their diversified portfolio of securities, presented less risk to investors than alternative investments in individual securities. It is significant, however, that in most instances investments in any one of the majority of stocks most favored by odd-lot investors would have yielded higher proceeds than the median mutual fund investment. Thus, in most instances the benefits of portfolio diversification and professional management afforded by a mutual fund investment were completely offset by the higher costs of the fund investment. This was especially true in investments of shorter duration where the high initial cost of investing in mutual funds had its greatest impact.

Investment performance, of course, can be measured and compared in many different ways. In some studies the average fund investor may fare as well or better than the average investor in an individual stock. Even in these instances, the mutual fund investor tends to pay dearly for any such advantages.[21]

Charles H. Thomas, director of the Aggressive Growth Funds Report, of Los Altos, California, an advisory service specializing in no-load funds, claims that the size of a fund's assets has a crucial bearing on its performance. In Thomas's opinion:

. . . no fund manager can effectively maneuver through the smaller, more efficient, faster growing segments of the market when he is hindered by oversized investments. The very best fund managers become bogged down beyond about the $100-million asset size, and the figure is lower for the manager with limited experience. We limit our new recommendations of funds to those under $100-million asset size.

However, this limit leaves plenty of latitude because only a few no-loads have more than $100 million in assets.

Such an approach, Thomas says, has produced "definitely superior" results. Since the service was started, in January, 1964, the average fund on his recommended list increased 88 percent, as compared to a 55 percent average increase for all mutual funds and a 42 percent gain for the Dow-Jones industrials.

Although Thomas's approach demonstrates the contrary, large funds theoretically should perform better than small ones. The advantages that size confers upon a corporation should not be overlooked. As the SEC Institutional Investor Study Report observed:

> Important economies can be realized by managing larger amounts. There are obvious administrative and management economies in employing specialized personnel to perform diverse tasks of marketing, trading, research, and portfolio management.
>
> Many cost items akin to overhead can be spread as fund size increases: e.g., visits to companies considered as potential investments are an important part of the institutional investors' research which small funds are generally unable to afford. These economies have been well documented. One study of mutual funds revealed that funds with assets over $400 million achieved per unit cost 50 percent lower than funds with assets below $5 million.
>
> There are other potential gains. Larger companies have greater leverage in buying research or other market information from brokerage houses because they generate large commissions. The absence of sufficient taper in commission rates for large transactions provides an obvious opportunity for those making large block trades to receive this sort of nonprice transfer in exchange for their commission business. As in any regulated market where prices and costs diverge, the competitive response is that of service or product competition and various nonprice transfers.[22]

On the other hand, the study report noted it is equally true that large funds have little or no size advantage in dealing in low-capitalization stocks.

The "size of the market" in any stock will limit the amount of money any given investor can place in a stock without reducing his own liquidity or the flexibility to sell his position. The capitalization of the company and how closely the stock is held help determine the size of the market in a stock. A large fund may have to diversify its portfolio very widely when investing in small companies. Large funds apparently enjoy no scale economies in investing small amounts in many issues.

The report concludes:

. . . the potential economies and market advantage of large funds have not been realized in practice. Invariably those with large amounts to manage have conceded some degree of market flexibility by reason of their size. One common tendency is to deal in the larger companies, which reduces average expected returns. The largest accumulations of funds have also tended to be less active in the market. Among mutual funds there is an inverse correlation of turnover rates with fund size. This is not to suggest high turnover as an end in itself, but rather to indicate that the larger fund accumulations are pursuing a different market strategy.[23]

Although smaller funds often do better than the larger ones, they too have potentially crippling limitations. The benefits of professional management enjoyed by the shareholders of some small funds may be quite meager; since most funds allocate no more than .5 percent of their total annual assets for an investment adviser, a fund with total assets of $1 million could pay only $5,000 a year, and one with $3 million in assets only $15,000 for this purpose — hardly enough to pay the salary of a competent office manager. The truth is that the portfolios of many small funds receive no more continual supervision than do the portfolios of many small individual investors.

A 1966 government study of investment companies lent further support to this conclusion. It found:

In some small funds, management depends almost entirely upon the acumen of a single individual who not only manages the fund's portfolio but performs a variety of administrative functions for the fund and sells its shares. In such situations, independent research and field visits to portfolio companies or those considered for inclusion in portfolios are seldom feasible, and the investment adviser necessarily relies heavily for investment research on information contained in company financial reports, standard financial manuals, and investment advisory materials generally distributed by brokerage houses.[24]

In view of the inadequate financial compensation on this level, the quality of advice rendered to small funds tends to be low, and the turnover among advisers, high. Not infrequently, when a fund's board of directors finds itself without an adviser for a long stretch, it begins making investment decisions on its own. A director of one fund — a lawyer without investment experience — told this author that at one such meeting the adviserless board considered investment suggestions based on a clipping in the *New York Daily News*, a conversation with a barber, and a report that "they" were buying oil stocks.

Do Funds Get Good Advice?

A puzzling aspect of the funds' inability to outperform the averages is that they do indeed receive investment information often denied the small investor. Everyone knows, of course, that when advice is handed out, the person who buys in lots of a few hundred shares or less is at the end of the line. A broker with a "hot" stock will first try to interest institutions, for that is the source of the big commissions. As the institutions buy, the price of the stock begins to rise. By the time the information trickles down to the small investor, the buyer is forced to pay high prices. The institutions can then sell at a profit.

Although they are supposed to provide the same information to all investors, officials of publicly held corporations willingly open doors to institutional portfolio managers that remain closed to the public. As a result of this practice, fund managers often have contacts with corporation directors and officers who are in a position to drop a few significant and potentially profitable words. Moreover, professional managers theoretically have the time to visit corporation plants and to examine annual reports and prospectuses and the training to make sense of what they see.

In a 1971 survey of small investors the *Wall Street Journal* found widespread disenchantment with the quality of investment advice made available to the general public. The *Journal's* nationwide poll of 1,000 Americans earning $10,000 or more a year revealed that 28 percent of those who had made market transactions in the previous two years indicated a lack of interest in reinvesting in stocks. Forty-six percent of investors who had not traded in two years also reported no desire to reinvest. Thirty-seven percent of all investors surveyed had negative opinions about the market as a place to invest their money, and 43 percent of these said that the market had become too dangerous for the small investor.[25]

In recent years, moreover, small investors have been selling substantially more stock than they have bought. Figures on odd-lot transactions (those of fewer than 100 shares) for most of 1971 showed that small investors sold two shares for every one bought.

According to the *Wall Street Journal*, the case of the Fairchild Camera and Instrument Corporation serves to illustrate why small investors think that they play the role of fourth-class citizens in the securities marketplace. In January, 1971, C. Lester Hogan, president of Fairchild, spoke at a meeting in New York arranged by Mabon, Nugent, and Company, a securities firm representing several institutional clients. Hogan told the listeners attending the private meeting that in 1970 Fairchild finished in a strong financial position and that the previous month's incoming orders were the best in ten months.

Apparently the institutions acted. In the seven trading days after the meeting, Fairchild common stock climbed from $24.50 to $32.65 a share.

The first reports of this meeting to reach the general public appeared February 4 — too late for small investors to participate in the price rise.

This was not the first time Hogan had had a private meeting with institutions. On October 29, 1969, he reportedly told institutional clients of William D. Witter, Inc., a New York securities concern, that sales had turned down that month. The stock dropped $2.125 a share the next day on a heavy volume of 326,500 shares. The following day the price fell $2.625 more on a volume of 97,200 shares. Neither the statement about the

October sales nor any explanation for the stock's decline reached the public until November 4 — six days after the private meeting.[26]

Of course, getting to the president of a corporation, who hands out information straight from the horse's mouth, is no surefire way to investment riches. The contrary is often true. Consider the National Student Marketing fiasco of 1968-1969. Uncritically accepting the confidential reports from its president about fantastic future earnings growth, mutual funds invested heavily in NSM stock in those years and helped to push its price per share from $3 to $68. When the earnings claimed in NSM's annual report turned out to include figures for companies that had not even been acquired yet, and when the presidential predictions for earnings growth proved to be wildly inflated, NSM stock fell as fast as it had risen. By early 1972 it hovered around $1.75.

The funds' advantage in reaching people with presumed superior knowledge *should* enable them to achieve better results, but often it does not. Why not?

As the NSM example indicates, much of the advice that mutual fund managers get firsthand is not worth getting at all. In a previous book, *If They're So Smart, How Come You're Not Rich?*, this author investigated the performance of the investment advisory industry and concluded, on the basis of the record, that brokerage house analysts and others who offer investment advice are, on the average, no better at choosing outstanding stocks than a person who throws darts at a stock market listing. Nor are they more successful in predicting market turns than the gambler who flips a coin to decide whether prices will rise or fall.

Such a dim view of the quality of professional advice available to the public (whether an institutional manager or the buyer of ten shares) is widely shared by Wall Streeters themselves. Recently Dan Dorfman, the influential columnist for the *Wall Street Journal*, interviewed Richard McKenzie, president of the Afuture Fund, on this subject.

According to McKenzie, three out of every four analysts providing tips to fund managers are incompetent — and even that figure may be too generous. Too many are reporters rather than analysts. "Too many use the broad-brush approach and fail to dig out the nitty-gritty details that really count when making an investment decision," said McKenzie.

As do other investors, mutual fund managers often witness the analysts' conflict of interest in action. McKenzie has found that some analysts' recommendations to buy are prompted less by consideration of investment merits than by the desire to generate orders. One factor, he adds, that influences a buy recommendation may be that the analyst *owns* the stock in question.

He cited two stocks that were bought as a result of supposedly strong research: Amrep (American) and Professional Golf (over-the-counter). "I saw Amrep plummet from the $60 to the teens level and Pro Golf, from 22 to 6. Of course, I'm responsible for the decision. But I learned the names of two more analysts to avoid."[27]

Strictly scientific evidence to support the view that mutual funds are often ill-served by their advisers is difficult to find. However, an attempt to compile such evidence was undertaken by R.E. Diefenbach, vice-president and director of research of the United States and Foreign Securities Corporation. In November, 1967, Diefenbach began to monitor all suggestions that his firm received from brokers.

Diefenbach included in his compilation all specific recommendations to buy or sell a stock received during the 80-week period from November 17, 1967, to May 23, 1969. Repeated recommendations from the same source to buy the same stock were regarded as separate recommendations, but not more often than once every 4 weeks. Diefenbach then measured the performance of the recommended stocks over a 52-week period, starting with its closing price on the Friday of the week in which the recommendation was received. He compared this performance with Standard and Poor's index of 425 industrial stocks for the same period.

Overall, he received 1,209 buy recommendations from 24 sources. While a majority of recommendations from 12 of these sources performed better than Standard and Poor's index, a majority of the recommendations from the 12 other sources did worse. In sum, only 47 percent of the recommendations did better than the S and P index, although the mean performance gain was 2.7 percent better.

Conforming to the tendency of brokerage firms to avoid sell recommendations, only 6 sources provided these. Only 46 sell recommendations were made — one for every 26 buy recommendations. (Diefenbach attributes analysts' reluctance to recommend selling a stock to the long-term upward trend of stocks in general, their fear of angering a valued management contact or corporate client, and the fact that sell recommendations affect only existing holders of a stock whereas everyone potentially can act upon a buy suggestion.) Of the sell recommendations received only 26 percent declined more than the S and P index. In 74 percent of the cases stocks that the funds were urged to sell actually held up better than the average. In general, the sell suggestions did 11.2 percent worse than the S and P index.

In discussing results of his study, Diefenbach concluded:

> We were unable *anywhere* . . . to find that quality of excellence so often claimed for institutional research. [They were] not among the most highly articulate merchandisers of this elusive quality. Not among those who coordinate the stock-selection process with economic analysis. And not among the proponents of the "star system" of independent analysts with large followings.[28]

Differences between the way mutual funds and individual investors get their investment ideas are not as significant as might be expected. Brokerage firms seeking institutional business must have employees who can effectively suggest stocks to buy. Regardless of what title these employees are given, they are indeed salespeople. Since many mutual fund managers want to meet with brokerage house employees who have personally done the basic research on a security, the one to whom they speak may also be an analyst. But as the research director of one brokerage firm put it: "The best analyst in the business who can't get his ideas across might as well be dead." As in merchandising, where the best products may wither on the shelves unless they are effectively promoted, here, too, the emphasis falls on the person who can produce orders. Consequently, the quality of investment suggestions may be pushed into second place.

Some Corporations Are Too Complex

One explanation for the funds' failure to perform well raises more questions than it answers. According to this explanation, it is incredibly difficult, if not virtually impossible, to understand what is going on in some large corporations. For example, consider the Penn Central fiasco: even as that line was rocketing to bankruptcy, scores of investment analysts were recommending its stock as a turnaround situation. Only five months before its financial collapse, Howard Butcher III, former director of Penn Central and head of a prestigious Philadelphia brokerage firm, publicly described Penn Central as the best candidate for substantial capital gain that he knew, a stock that could increase its current price fivefold.[29] Instead, of course, the stock plummeted. There is no reason to doubt later explanations by Butcher and other analysts that they were never aware of the corporation's real financial condition. Yet representatives of the railroad maintain that the figures revealing its plight could have been easily located in Penn Central's voluminous reports to the Securities and Exchange Commission, the Interstate Commerce Commission, and other governmental agencies.

An article in *Fortune* magazine stated:

> There has long been a formal presumption that investors can form judgments about the value of corporate securities by examining the registration statements and annual reports filed by public corporations. The presumption has always been something of a fiction as far as most individual investors are concerned. In the past, however, it was at least possible for trained analysts to make something of the reports. Now, in part because of the monstrously involved financing associated with some of the conglomerates, the capability has been called into question. It is an observable fact that security analysts disagree among themselves about the value of those packages of debentures, stock, and warrants offered investors by conglomerates on the prowl. One well-known investment banker acknowledged that he no longer had any clear notions about the value of a well-known conglomerate in which, he also acknowledged, his firm had a sizable

interest; he added that it seemed quite unlikely that the company's own management was any clearer.

The problem, then, is that the Street suddenly finds itself marketing a fair number of securities about which investors are simply unable to form reasonable opinions. The solution is not entirely clear but will surely involve a thorough overhauling of disclosure rules; it might also involve prohibitions on certain types of securities.[30]

The Hazards of Group-Think

According to one highly regarded analyst, Bradbury K. Thurlow, defects are inherent to the process by which some funds reach buy-sell decisions — that is, through the deliberations of the investment committee. In effect, Thurlow maintains:

> . . . as often as not, the individual members of the committee will have widely differing and irreconcilable views on investment strategy and will find that their areas of general agreement are those in which they feel least competent to express their own views. Thus the element of individual talent tends to be submerged in the homogenized mediocrity of "group think."
>
> An additional problem peculiar to mutual funds arises from the competition with other funds and the publicity given their transactions. An "odd-ball" fund that buys an unfashionable stock and subsequently loses money will inevitably be subjected to criticism, while a dozen funds that lose just as much money in a respectable or fashionable stock will be above reproach. This situation has led to mass blunders in investment judgment that not only lost money for the mutual funds involved, but had far wider repercussions since they were piously followed by the public at large. It is seriously to be questioned whether the "growth stock" mania of 1960-1961 would ever have attained the disastrous proportions it reached had it not been for the publicity given to the investment tactics of the growth funds and the enthusiastic support they received from Wall Street research departments.[31]

About Inside Information

Although inside information itself has never proved to be a consistently reliable guide to investment policy (Bernard Baruch said, "Enough inside information could sink the Bank of

England"), many mutual fund managers find it difficult to resist the temptations to act (with other people's money, to be sure) not on the facts but on rumors about corporate developments of which the public is not yet aware.

Many managers consciously attempt to get the rumors before the facts. And there are shreds of wisdom to this approach. Stock prices are fueled primarily to expectations, and rumors that feed such expectations often will raise prices as effectively as concrete developments. However, trading on rumors involves two risks: first (and, many Wall Streeters think, most importantly) is the hazard of hearing the rumors late, after others have heard and acted and are ready to extract their profits. The second hazard is that the rumor may be denied. To the speculator the truth of the rumor is irrelevant.

In his classic treatise, *The General Theory of Employment, Interest and Money,* John Maynard Keynes described the investing game as follows:

> The actual, private object of the most skilled investment today is "to beat the gun," as the Americans so well express it, to outwit the crowd, and to pass the bad, or depreciating, half-crown to the other fellow.
>
> The battle of wits . . . does not even require gulls among the public to feed the maws of the professional; it can be played by the professionals amongst themselves . . . for it is, so to speak, a game of Snap, of Old Maid, of Musical Chairs — a pastime in which he is victor who says Snap neither too soon nor too late, who passes the Old Maid to his neighbor before the game is over, who secures a chair for himself when the music stops.[32]

Curran W. Harvey, portfolio manager of the T. Rowe Price Growth Stock Fund, fully agrees that a major problem afflicting performance funds is their tendency to "buy" stories. As Harvey puts it:

> A friend of mine went to a very much-in-demand performance fund to do research. He quickly learned that checking out a story did not signify visiting management, and the like, to find out if the story was true. What it meant was to find out how many people on the Street had heard it, because if too many people had

acted on the story already, the stock's price would have discounted it.

A lot of people have ended up as long-term investors in companies with good stories but lousy fundamentals. There may be bad management, a lousy product, or just no substance to the story in the first place. When people lose interest in the story, there may be nothing left.[33]

So How Come They're Experts?

The funds' generally unimpressive performance record raises questions about two practices that cast fund managers in the role of omniscient experts.

The first, a practice followed by some individual investors, consists of basing investment decisions on what the funds in general (or one fund in particular) are buying or selling. Individuals do less of this today than they did in the early sixties. *Following the funds*, buying what they have bought because they "must know what they're doing," has produced mediocre results. One reason for this lack of success is that the funds frequently buy and sell within extremely short time frameworks. Suppose you discover in June that the New Era Fund has held 25,000 shares of Homestake Mining since March 31, and you decide that what is good for New Era is good for you. What you probably do not know is that the fund already has made its targeted profit — or uncovered information that has caused it to change its mind about the stock — and has sold its shares on April 15. You become a follower without a leader. Moreover, as established earlier in this chapter, funds do not get superior investment advice from their sources of information, nor do they come up with outstanding investment ideas on their own.

The second dubious practice, one in which most financial publications heartily engage, is to quote opinions of mutual fund managers about the market as though: (a) the managers have superior information; and (b) they will freely tell the public what they know.

At any given time you can read in one publication or another what the manager of the XYZ Fund thinks the next market move will be and which stocks will lead it. It cannot be emphasized too strongly that *to act on such forecasts is to invite great risk.*

Initially it should be noted that the "experts" quoted on the financial pages are not necessarily investment managers with superior records. They are experts first because they have a title, not necessarily for any other reason. The press generally looks for interesting copy, so the fund executive who speaks colorfully and well — despite an abominable track record — will often be quoted at greater length than the dry, colorless manager who does a better job for the fund's shareholders. Some financial writers think that anybody who runs a fund *must* be an expert and therefore utters words that carry weight. Therefore, when you read what an "expert" thinks about the market, do not automatically assume that the newspaper has checked out the credentials and record of the reporter. Do not assume that the opinions of the writer are worth serious consideration.

More important to remember is the fact that *any* fund manager is unlikely to hand out consistently good advice via the press. If the manager gives an interview to a newspaper, this thought probably runs through the executive's mind: "Why should I say anything to hurt my own position in the market?"

Why indeed? The manager owes nothing to the general public. Obligation is only to the shareholders, and the manager acts accordingly. A fund's operations are such that it will rarely have less than 80 percent of its assets invested in stocks and bonds. (As a group, funds usually keep more than 90 percent of their assets invested.) Invariably, therefore, it stands to gain from a rise in market prices. And, of course, a fund manager wants the fund's assets to go up: the manager's fees rise accordingly. Since the manager derives no advantage from predicting a decline in prices, a manager who encourages the public to sell jeopardizes his or her own income and the value of the manager's portfolio. Conversely, the executive will hardly recommend stocks "due for a rise" — and thereby push up their prices — unless the manager has already bought all he or she intends to acquire. It is equally naive to assume that a manager will publicly criticize any personally owned stock: instinct dictates the sale of personally owned stock before encouraging you to sell yours. (If the selling public pushes the price low enough, the manager may buy again.)

By the nature of things, therefore, fund managers are almost invariably bullish when talking for public consumption. The most they usually concede is that the market is temporarily "overbought" and due for a mild correction before it resumes its upward advance. If the manager is more bearish than that, irate shareholders would almost certainly demand to know why the general public was advised to sell while the manager failed to sell the shares he was paid to manage.

Realistically, it should be remembered that fund managers have no obligation whatsoever to you, the public. Their obligation is to their shareholders. Consequently, they will tell you only what helps the interests of their shareholders. They will certainly not suggest that you take any action that will adversely affect the asset value of their fund, and hence the fortunes of their own shareholders. Should managers, in a rare burst of candor, recommend that you pursue an investment policy that would hurt their shareholders, they would face a barrage of criticism.

Since fund managers' forecasts tend to be primarily bullish, they are accurate on occasion; doubtless they predict bull markets more accurately than falling ones. But do not count on a fund manager to tell you that a bear market is about to begin or will continue. It simply is not in the interest of a manager to be a bear in public.

Actually the records show that at certain market points you are better off doing the opposite of what the funds do. In general, when they have fully invested their money (presumably in expectation of higher prices), you should be ready to sell; when they have substantial cash reserves (presumably in fear of lower prices), you would do better to buy.

For example, the 1970 bear market bottomed on May 26. It might be assumed that at this point the professional managers would have fully invested their money, thereby taking advantage of the numerous bargains available. However, the monthly asset report released by the Investment Company Institute showed that on May 31 the cash held by the funds amounted to an all-time high — 13.4 percent of assets. Instead of providing stability to a panicking market, the funds contributed to the plunge by selling $130 million more securities than they bought.

This was not the first time they had badly misjudged the market's direction. More often than not, their cash reserves have been low at stock market highs (for example, 6.1 percent in December, 1968; 5.8 percent in 1966; 4.3 percent in 1961). Conversely, reserves usually have been highest at bear market bottoms (9.7 percent in October, 1966; 6.3 percent in November, 1962). The professional managers thus join the odd-lotters in sharing the description: "They're always wrong."

4

The Closed Circle of
Mutual Fund Management

I<small>T</small> is important to realize that there is nothing magical about mutual funds or the people who run them. There is no legal requirement that mutual funds be operated by experienced "professional management," and nothing about them necessarily insures that they will achieve better results than your corner broker or even your neighborhood barber. True, most big funds (those commonly sold through their own sales organizations or by brokerage houses) retain experienced advisers to select their portfolios. But according to law this need not be so. It has not been rare to find funds organized and managed by individuals whose qualifications to handle their own investments, much less other people's, are suspect.

In 1967 a lawyer (I will call him Joe) discovered that some of the stocks he had purchased within the past year on the basis of random tips were doing remarkably well. A stock purchased for 12 was now 33, while another stock had climbed from 6 to 28. Other stocks had doubled in price. Though Joe had never paid much attention to investing before, he began to consider himself an astute investor with an inborn knack for picking winners. (He had not yet heard the axiom, "Genius is a rising stock market.") At the end of the year he noted that his assets had increased 93 percent — a better record than that of most funds. He looked into the mechanics of fund management and found that it could be a profitable enterprise indeed. Not only could fund organizers assure themselves of the contract to manage its portfolio; there was also the possibility of a golden windfall if the management company itself were sold to others. Together with his two law partners and other business associates he applied to the Securities and Exchange Commission for permission to operate a fund and seek shareholders. This process of applying is time-consuming. It generally requires the services of an attorney, whose fees might run as high as $50,000. Joe and his associates did the work themselves and saved the fees. In eight months they received clearance to operate what I will call the Bartholomew Fund.

The Bartholomew Fund started its operations with 60,000 shares of stock outstanding, $600,000 in assets, and Joe tirelessly preaching that stock prices were sure to rise. Persons of limited means were encouraged to take their money out of their "stodgy" savings accounts and purchase shares in the fund. Gains of 50 or even 100 percent a year were presented as realistic investment goals.

For a few months prices rose fast, but expectations rose even faster. The fund hired a publicity man, and soon Joe's analysis of the state of the market appeared in the local newspapers. The rising asset value per share attracted wide notice. People began calling to find out whom they had to know to buy some of the fund's shares.

All things must end, and for Joe the beginning of the end came in December, 1968. The analysts originally called the general market decline a correction, but they were wrong. By May, 1970, the Bartholomew Fund's gains had melted like snow in August. The fund's assets per share plummeted from a high point of $17.42 to a low of $4.47. Shareholders panicked and redeemed shares. Joe's partners deserted him. When his own heady paper profits turned into ruinous losses, he too sold out and deactivated the fund. "I'm cured," he announced. But as the market turned up and plus signs multiplied in the stock listing tables, he began thinking of starting up again. And no law prohibits him from doing so.

You Too Can Start a Mutual Fund

It takes almost nothing — nothing but nerve and legal know-how (or the money to hire it) — to obtain the legal right to organize and operate a mutual fund.

Most funds are set up, of course, to provide the maximum advantage to those who do the setting up. This fact conforms to a universal law: "Institutions exist for their own benefit primarily and only secondarily for those they pretend to serve."

You might expect organizers of a fund to hire the best people available to manage their portfolios. And organizers claim this is exactly what they do. It is remarkable, however, that the best men and women available are invariably the organizers themselves. For the most part funds are organized by individuals who intend to hire "independent contractors" to manage the portfolios. Their primary motive in establishing a fund often is to give themselves a job. And, as we shall see, it is a very lucrative job indeed.

A separate entity, known as an investment adviser, is set up to manage the fund portfolio. The fund pays the adviser an advisory fee. Traditionally, this fee has been .5 percent of the fund's average net assets during the year, although under some fee schedules this rate remains in effect only up to a stipulated level; above that level a lower rate applies. The investment adviser selects the fund's portfolio and operates or supervises most other aspects of its business.

Most advisers also supply the funds they manage with office space as well as the clerks and accountants needed to carry on the fund's business. In most cases such services are paid for by the usual advisory fee. A 1966 study by the SEC noted that although the typical fund has a board of directors and one or more executive officers, "A substantial portion of the fund's directors and all, or virtually all, of its officers will normally be associated with or employed by its advisers. In most cases all of the compensation that such persons receive for their services to the fund is paid to them by the adviser, not by the fund."[1]

A mutual fund investment adviser can be an individual, but most advisers are either partnerships or corporations. Although many advisers affiliated with the large funds have no nonfund clients, some combine their mutual fund activities with a general investment counseling and/or securities business.

The law does not specify qualifications for the investment advisers of a mutual fund — almost anyone can qualify. It is not necessary even to register with the SEC, a requirement that is mandatory for advisers who deal with the public. (According to the law, only investment advisers with more than fifteen advisory clients or with a public advisory practice must be registered.)

Life in a Goldfish Bowl

Mutual funds and other investment companies are regulated by the SEC under the Investment Company Act of 1940. Many fund managers complain that the public disclosures required by this act force them to operate in a goldfish bowl. To a large extent this is true, and for good reason. The history of investment trusts in the United States prior to enactment of this act is not one to inspire confidence in their integrity when left to their own devices.

The Investment Company Act followed an exhaustive study of the then infant investment company industry, undertaken by the SEC at the direction of Congress. At that time the SEC reported itself alarmed at the extent to which investment companies had been operated in the interests of their managers and to the detriment of investors. An SEC report stated:

> A high incidence of recklessness and improvidence was noted. Insiders often viewed investment companies as sources of capital for business ventures of their own and as captive markets for unsalable securities that they, the insiders, wished to convert into cash. Controlling persons frequently took unfair advantage of the companies in other ways, often using broad exculpatory clauses to insulate them from liability for their wrongdoing. Outright larceny and embezzlement were not uncommon. Managers were able to buy investment company shares for less than net asset value, thus enriching themselves at the shareholders' expense.
>
> In addition, reports to shareholders were often misleading and

deceptive. Controlling positions in investment companies — represented by special classes of stock or by advisory contracts — were bought and sold without the consent, or even the knowledge, of public shareholders. Basic investment policies were changed without shareholders approval. The advisory contracts themselves were often long term and either noncancellable or cancellable only upon the payment of a substantial penalty by the company.

As a consequence of the Investment Trust Study, Congress concluded that the "completely liquid, mobile, and readily negotiable" assets of investment companies offered unusual opportunities to the unscrupulous and that disclosure alone was an inadequate safeguard for shareholders. Congress said further:

> The national public interest and the interest of investors are adversely affected . . . when investment companies are organized, operated, managed, or their portfolio securities are selected in the interest of directors, officers, investment advisers, depositors, or other affiliated persons thereof in the interest of underwriters, brokers or dealers, in the interest of special classes of their security holders, or in the interest of other investment companies or persons engaged in other lines of business, rather than in the interest of all classes of security holders.[2]

The Investment Company Act of 1940 established a broad regulatory system aimed at correcting inequitable capital structures and dishonesty and loans to unfair property with insiders. However, the act specifically excluded regulation of compensation for services — sales loads, managerial compensation, and brokerage commissions. Here fund managers retained a very large measure of discretion. It was thought that internal company regulation through certain shareholder approval provisions and provisions governing the composition of investment companies' boards of directors would check abuses in these areas. As we shall see, this was a monumental miscalculation.

In common with other securities acts, the Investment Company Act requires registration of security offerings. Investment companies (and in some cases their promoters and underwriters) are prohibited from engaging in interstate commerce and from using the mails unless the company is registered with the SEC. Willful violation of the registration provisions is a federal crime. Registered investment companies are required to make periodic reports to the commission and to their stockholders.

Much of the act is intended to protect shareholders from outright dishonesty. It bars from the investment company industry persons convicted of, or enjoined from committing, certain types of misconduct involving security transactions. The act makes larceny, conversion, or embezzlement of investment company assets a federal crime and authorizes the commission to obtain injunctions against "gross misconduct or gross abuse of trust" by persons associated with registered investment companies. The commission is authorized to prescribe the accounting policies and practices of registered investment companies. Financial statements must be certified by independent public accountants whose selection must be ratified by the stockholders. Further, the commission is authorized to establish bonding requirements for those having access to monies and securities of investment companies and to prescribe rules to protect investment company portfolio securities.

Finding that "complex, multitiered capital structures characterized by thin substrata of equity beneath towers of indebtedness" had proved damaging to investment company shareholders in the past, the act provided that closed-end companies may not issue debt securities unless they have an asset coverage of 300 percent and cannot issue preferred stock unless such stock has an asset coverage of at least 200 percent. They cannot issue more than one class of preferred stock. Open-end companies may not issue any debt securities.

The commission has the power to prevent investment companies from buying securities on margin or selling them short. All stock issued by a management investment company, whether open-end or closed-end, must be voting stock. The extent to which registered investment companies can invest in securities of other registered investment companies, insurance companies, brokers or dealers in securities, underwriters, distributors of securities, and investment advisers is restricted.

To check the heretofore virtually unrestricted power of management groups, the act requires that at least 40 percent of a board of directors must consist of persons who are neither officers nor employees of the investment company and who are unaffiliated with its investment adviser. However, *unaffiliated* does not mean *unrelated*. Result: unaffiliated directors sometimes are relatives or close friends of their affiliated colleagues. And a director may own as much as 4.9 percent of the outstanding voting securities of an investment adviser without becoming affiliated with the adviser.

The act also provides that if any of the investment company's officers, directors, or employees are investment bankers or affiliated with investment bankers, a majority of the board must consist of persons who are neither investment bankers nor affiliated with investment bankers.

Transactions in which investment companies lend money to sell or buy property from investment advisers, principal underwriters, and other affiliated persons are prohibited without SEC approval. Such approval can be granted only if the commission finds that "Terms of the proposed transaction, including the consideration to be paid or received, are reasonable and fair and do not involve overreaching on the part of any person concerned."

The act guards against insiders purchasing investment company shares on more favorable terms than those available to the general public. Subject to certain exceptions, mutual fund shares may be sold only at a public offering price described in the prospectus. If insiders profit from short-term trading in the securities of a closed-end investment company, the profits can be demanded by the company.

When the act was written, it was recognized that in promoting fund expansion, the adviser may channel sales, and thus brokerage commissions generated by the fund's portfolio transactions to retail dealers who recommend and sell the fund's shares. Such a course of broker compensation may be at the cost of minimizing brokerage costs. However, Congress in 1940 was of the view that "a few elementary safeguards" would sufficiently protect the public interest in the areas of advisory fees, underwriting compensation, and brokerage commissions. The "elementary safeguards" imposed by the act are two in number. The act regulates the form and content of advisory and underwriting contracts. It further stipulates the manner in which unaffiliated directors and shareholders must approve these contracts.

The act requires that the investment company's contract with its adviser be in writing and that the adviser's compensation be described with precision. Before an advisory contract can become effective, it must be approved by holders of a majority of the fund's outstanding voting securities. If the contract is to continue in effect more than two years subsequent to the date of its execution, such continuance must be specifically approved annually by either (a) the board of directors as a whole, including a majority of unaffiliated directors or (b) the vote of the holders of a majority of the outstanding voting securities.

The act sets no express limits on compensation paid to affiliated persons, nor does it expressly require that such compensation be "reasonable." The SEC asserts its jurisdiction to order changes only when managerial "emoluments" are so excessive as to constitute "gross misconduct or gross abuse of trust" and it becomes necessary that the affiliate be suspended or barred from investment companies.

Different provisions govern agreements between funds and their principal underwriters. Underwriting agreements must be approved by either the board of directors, including a majority of unaffiliated directors, or the holders of a majority of outstanding voting securities. In contrast, advisory contracts can be approved only by holders of a majority of the outstanding voting securities. And although a fund can terminate an advisory contract at any time, it has no such right to terminate an underwriting agreement.

Explicit provisions regulate sales loads in contractual plans. The aggregate sales load charged in the sale of such plans cannot exceed 9 percent of the total payments to be made, and no more than one-half of the first year's payments or their equivalent can be deducted as a commission.

There are no specific ceilings on the sales loads funds generally may charge. However, the act expresses opposition to "unconscionable or grossly excessive" sales loads, and it authorizes the SEC and the National Association of Securities Dealers (NASD) to implement that policy by appropriate rules.

The act contains no provisions regulating the manner in which investment companies may distribute the brokerage business generated by their portfolio activities.

In a formal appraisal of the act made in 1966, the SEC observed:

> The provisions designed to protect investment companies and their shareholders from exploitation by irresponsible persons and to prevent inequitable or discriminatory capital structures as well as the safeguards against more subtle forms of overreaching through self-dealing transactions between investment companies and their affiliated persons have worked well on the whole. However, many of the act's provisions were specifically tailored to meet conditions and practices prevalent in the investment company industry of a generation ago. And some of these provisions are not suited to contemporary needs. Experience has shown that there are ambiguities and anomalies in the act that should be corrected.
>
> Because of the salutary provisions of the act, serious abuses in transactions between investment companies and their affiliated persons have been reduced to a minimum. While persons affiliated with investment companies may still obtain substantial benefits by virtue of their relationships to the companies, those benefits come not from the exploitation of investment company assets, but mainly from compensation for furnishing managerial, brokerage, and, in the case of mutual funds, underwriting services to the companies. Hence the act has achieved one of its principal aims: to make investment company management a skilled and an honorable profession.[3]

Nevertheless, other studies made under SEC auspices questioned the adequacy of the protections afforded investors by the act with regard to advisory fees, sales compensations, and brokerage commissions. These questions were brought to the fore by the unforeseen growth of the mutual fund industry. Sales loads, advisory fees, and brokerage commissions may not have provided substantial emoluments in the $.5-billion mutual fund industry of 1940, but they are most significant in the $55-billion industry of today. Total advisory fees paid by the funds amount to some $275 million a year, and mutual fund portfolio transactions generate $200 million of brokerage commissions annually.

In practice, the elementary safeguards failed to provide effective control over the size of the investment advisory fees and other forms of remuneration received by those who sponsor, manage, and distribute the shares of mutual funds. With few exceptions the unaffiliated directors have other businesses that occupy their time. Most of them do what the fund managers want. They serve mainly as window dressing.

Consequently, instead of the fund's controlling the adviser, the adviser usually controls the fund. In one report the SEC noted:

Where unaffiliated directors have sought to become more active in the negotiation process, lack of competition among advisers and the dependence of the fund on its adviser for continuing and constant advisory and other services have made effective negotiation between unaffiliated directors and the adviser over advisory fees an unrealistic expectation. It is the adviser, not the fund, which over a period of years has developed the organization necessary to manage the fund's portfolio and to furnish it with many, and in some cases all, of the non-advisory services required for its operation, including in many cases even the remuneration of the unaffiliated directors. The fund's dependence on this organization and the argument that many shareholders have invested in the fund on the strength of the adviser's reputation have made it unrealistic to expect that unaffiliated directors would seriously consider replacing the existing adviser with a new and untested organization simply because the adviser refused to agree to fee rates that reflect an equitable sharing of the economies of size. Nor is it feasible to expect the unaffiliated directors to recruit, train and manage a staff of internal advisers. Even if the unaffiliated directors, who in some cases are only a minority, and in many other cases are a bare majority, of the board of directors could obtain sufficient support among the directors for such drastic steps, it is unlikely that their action would be uncontested by the existing adviser. The adviser's interest in continuing its relationship with the fund necessarily and inevitably would lead it to devote considerable resources of its own in waging a proxy fight to retain that relationship and might even lead it to use the resources of the fund itself under a claim that it was in fact engaged in a contest over important management policy.

For these reasons, negotiations between unaffiliated directors and fund advisers over fees lack an essential element of arm's length bargaining — the threat of terminating negotiations and contracting with other parties. That such a threat does not exist is illustrated by an instance known to the commission in which the unaffiliated directors of a large fund considered severing its ties with the existing adviser. Preliminary inquiries directed to qualified advisers by the unaffiliated directors failed to elicit any interest in competing for the advisory contract with the fund's existing adviser. Nor were the unaffiliated directors able to exert pressure on the adviser to cause a reduction in fees — even in circumstances unusually favorable to such action. (The adviser later voluntarily put into effect a modest reduction of fees.) In our view, based on considerable exposure and experience with these situations, it is wholly unrealistic to expect controls over advisory fees to be effective unless there is an explicit legal standard applicable to the adviser and affiliated directors and an adequate procedure to insure adherence to that standard, neither of which is provided under existing law.[4]

Hamer Budge, chairman of the SEC in 1969, considered the organization of mutual funds both "peculiar" and "unique":

True, the fund itself looks — when viewed superficially — just like any other corporation. It has a board of directors, and it also has one or more executive officers. But, in the case of most funds, a substantial portion of the directors, and all or virtually all of its officers, are normally associated with or employed by the adviser. So for all practical purposes the typical fund is under the adviser's thumb. It was conceived by the adviser, and it never assumes a truly independent existence.

This pattern is commonly referred to as one of external management. It is the traditional way of doing things in the investment company field, but it is hard to conceive of anything like it anywhere else. There is no valid comparison between external management in the mutual fund business and the ordinary business practice of subcontracting. Mutual funds just do not go out to buy advisory and underwriting services on the open market on the best terms they can get. They are generally tied to their advisers. The adviser sets his price, and, typically, the fund pays that price. The arm's length bargaining element in the ordinary business relationship is completely lacking here.[5]

In 1967, Manuel E. Cohen, Budge's predecessor as SEC chairman, testified before a House committee that for the most part the "unusual management structure" of mutual funds caused no detrimental effects. He stated in part:

> To the extent that investors select the investment management of a particular adviser, they may expect that the adviser will be in a position to see that his policies and recommendations are carried out. It is important to remember, however, that with respect to the fixing of investment advisory or management fees and, in many cases, the charges for sales of fund shares to the public, an obvious conflict of interest exists between the fund managers who staff and control the fund and whose representatives sit on the board of the fund, on the one hand, and the shareholders on the other.
>
> The conflict between the adviser-director's duty to shareholders to keep advisory and other fees as low as possible, and his own self-interest in maximizing them, has an additional facet where the investment adviser is publicly owned, a situation which exists with respect to about twenty advisers to investment companies. These advisers are responsible for managing and furnishing investment advice with respect to about one-half of the total assets of the mutual fund industry. In the case of such a publicly-held adviser a duty to maximize its profits — at the expense of the fund — runs from those in control of the adviser to its own shareholders. Thus, the adviser's representative on the fund's board must constantly face pressures from the public shareholders of the investment adviser that conflict with his duties to the public shareholders of the fund.[6]

As Cohen pointed out, outside the public utility field prices of goods and charges for services are normally determined at arm's length by the forces of competition. Thus, in an ideal market the interaction of competing investment advisers, vying for the patronage of the various funds, might be relied upon to set the fee rates at a fair level, providing the funds with the services they require at a reasonable cost. However, such competitive forces, with respect to advisory fees, have not existed in the mutual fund industry.

New York attorney Abraham L. Pomerantz, prosecutor of more than a dozen stockholder suits against fund managements, has gained much insight into the way funds operate. It is, he says, foolish to think that the unaffiliated director is really independent. Pomerantz stated:

> Here you have conflict of interest unparalleled. It is only the independent director who stands between the advisers and their uninhibited acquisitiveness. So the independent director has a vital role to play. But he has not played it. The fact that in the long history of mutual funds no investment adviser has ever been fired is perhaps the most eloquent testimony to the supineness of the independent director. The fact is that these independent directors are handpicked by the advisory men — the men who need to be watched. And it is not surprising that they are not selected for, nor do they exhibit, fearlessness or truculence.[7]

Appearing before the Senate Committee on Banking and Currency in 1967, Pomerantz testified that he received precious little help from unaffiliated directors in his suits on behalf of stockholders. He was questioned by Senator Wallace F. Bennett, of Utah:

POMERANTZ: I know one man who to my knowledge really stood up as an unaffiliated director. When I tried to settle my lawsuit, he fought with me because he thought my proposed settlement wasn't adequate.
  . . . in the 14 cases I have run into, involving something like a hundred or more unaffiliated directors, I have not seen [his] counterpart . . . .
  These men, by and large, go along and rubberstamp.
  The proof is that when these funds were growing from $100 million to $2 billion and they were getting a flat one-half of one percent advisory fee, wouldn't you imagine that somewhere, sometime, somebody among the unaffiliated directors would say, "Now look, fellows, this is getting a little out of hand. A $500,000 fee is not a $10 million fee. Wouldn't it be nice if we were to sit around the table to talk about reducing it from half a percent to three-eighths. percent or some scale-down?" It never happened.
BENNETT: You're sure it never happened?
POMERANTZ: It never happened.
BENNETT: You're sure?
POMERANTZ: It never happened at the instigation of an unaffiliated director.[8]

Another myth, says Pomerantz, is that stockholders have real control over the fund's board of directors. Of this he says:

> Confronted with the challenge to the claim of excessiveness of the advisory fee, the classical ploy of the adviser is to plead that the shareholders of the mutual fund overwhelmingly approved or ratified the fee. They always do. And who is the plaintiff or his lawyer to interfere with the will of the shareholder in this exercise of corporate democracy? In effect, defendants say: Don't be like the apocryphal boy scout who insists on helping the old lady across the street — even though she doesn't want to go.
>
> Now the facts of life don't correspond to this theory of stockholder approval. For as any sophisticated lawyer or businessman or congressman knows, there is just about nothing in the world that a shareholder will fail to approve or ratify if asked to do so — and if there is no contest. Ratification can be had for the asking.
>
> Nonetheless, courts give to approval by so-called independent directors or by shareholders an importance which does not correspond to reality. Once defendants come forward with ratification, the courts put a huge, an almost impossible burden on the suing shareholder. He must now show that the fees are so large as to constitute not mere excessiveness but "waste." What is waste? Without attempting a definition, the courts have said that the fee must be so staggering as "to shock the conscience of the court." And many a case where the court felt that the fees were possibly excessive was dismissed because the excess was not great enough to shock its conscience.[9]

Because the unaffiliated directors have no practical alternative to accepting the proposals of the adviser, they have tended to regard renewal of the investment advisory contract as a matter of corporate routine, similar to rubber-stamping the minutes of a meeting. In several cases, the investment advisory contract of a mutual fund was not renewed as required by the Investment Company Act simply because those concerned *forgot* about it.[10]

Mutual fund defenders claim that the existing requirement of shareholder approval — requiring shareholders to approve the selection of an adviser — is adequate. It can be argued that this is analogous to telling the person who dislikes the service provided by the local telephone company to go start his own. Most shareholders sign and return their proxies when the management requests them to. There is little else they can do. Were they to vote down an investment advisory contract, the fund would be without an adviser, and their investments would be in jeopardy.

Of this situation the SEC said the following:

> It is commonly accepted, and many years of experience with proxy regulation in all areas of corporate life support the conclusion, that in the absence of organized opposition to a proposal, most shareholders either do not return their proxies or mark them in favor of management proposals. In the case of mutual funds the possibility of organized opposition is particularly unrealistic. Advisers do not compete for advisory contracts with funds by organizing proxy contests. And the possibility of a shareholder-initiated contest is also remote.[11]

The Making of a Mutual Fund

Before it may legally sell shares to the public, a mutual fund must complete two SEC procedures: the fund itself must be registered in compliance with the Investment Company Act of 1940, and the shares to be offered to the public must be registered in compliance with the Securities Act of 1933.

"Friends," it is rumored in Washington, get preferential treatment at the SEC. And, the rumor goes on, a little money placed in the right pockets can promote such friendship. Testifying before a House committee on December 10, 1969, Norman F. Dacey — acerbic critic of various fund practices — told this story:

> I have had a mutual fund in registration with the commission for 16 months, since August, 1968. I can learn nothing about its status. It does not have to take a long while for a mutual fund to be registered. I recently compiled a list of funds whose registrations have become effective this year. Some took 11 months, some 10, 9, 8. One fund, interestingly, became registered in 4 short months. It is sponsored by a company of which Richard Nixon was a director before he became president. The chairman of the Securities and Exchange Commission, appointed by

Mr. Nixon, was recently disclosed to be negotiating with this same sponsor for a top post with the company. I mention these facts only in passing. They are simply coincidental and, of course, had nothing to do with the remarkable speed with which the fund was registered.

I was advised by a knowledgeable attorney that if I hired an ex-SEC lawyer for a fee of $25,000 he would "walk" my registration papers through the commission in short order. The SEC is a revolving door between law school and a lucrative practice as "an attorney specializing in SEC matters" — which is simply a euphemism for influence peddling. I declined to pay any such bribe. I paid a $2,000 registration fee that entitled my application to fair consideration. It has not received that. Instead, immediately after I filed a shareholders' derivative action against Enterprise Fund and publicly criticized the commission for its handling of letter stock, my registration papers were twice mysteriously "lost" by the commission.

After the commission declined to take any action to protect Enterprise investors from the shareholder accounting mess, I told Herbert Milstein, a top enforcement official of the commission, that I would see if a committee of the Congress could do any better. A few days later two representatives of the commission appeared at my office upon the direct instructions of the enforcement division to ransack my files and make a special audit of my books.[12]

In registering its shares the fund is required by law to state the number of shares to be offered and the offering price and must pay to the SEC a fee equivalent to .0002 of their value. Thus the fee for a million shares offered at $15 amounts to $3,000. If the fund sells these shares and wishes to offer more, it may amend its registration statement to cover the additional shares.

Some states permit the intrastate sale of any funds registered with the SEC. Others follow a uniform securities law, with which issuers of stock must comply. Still others require corporations to go through individual registration before their shares may be sold. The registration papers generally must specify the number of shares to be sold within the state, and a fee similar to the federal fee must be paid for each unit.

To avoid excessive fees, fund organizers often underestimate sales expectations. But if they sell more shares than they have registered, they violate the law. Shareholders who have bought unregistered shares have the right to demand their money back with interest.

The registration of mutual fund shares under the Securities Act of 1933 is similar to the registration of other publicly held shares. But since mutual funds are consistently sold to the public, their shares are constantly *in registration*. Hence, when you first buy a fund's shares, you should receive a prospectus. Generally speaking, a prospectus is a statement of financial condition filed with the SEC. However, SEC approval of the prospectus means only that the prospectus seems to tell the truth and does not withhold important information. In fact, the prospectus must state that "these securities have not been approved or disapproved by the Securities and Exchange Commission nor has the commission passed upon the accuracy or adequacy of this prospectus. Any representation to the contrary is a criminal offense." However, the SEC will not approve any prospectus that does not seem to tell the whole truth about the corporation involved. The format of the prospectus is defined by law. Even the size of the type in which paragraphs and statements must be set is regulated.

The prospectus describes the fund's investment objectives. It cites the limitations to be placed on portfolio transactions and summarizes the fund's past portfolio turnover rate (if the fund has been in operation already) or, for new funds, the anticipated rate. The prospectus must also list various other shareholder arrangements — for example, sales charges, if any, levied against the shareholder who reinvests dividends. It must list the names and detail the backgrounds of the fund's directors and executive officers, and it must present audited reports of the company's financial condition and past investment record.

The prospectus must also tell how much of the investor's money goes to the underwriters. Usually the sales charge is divided between the principal underwriter and the dealer who retails the shares, except where the principal underwriter makes the retail sale. Then the principal underwriter retains the entire load. If the charge is divided, the underwriter gets from one-third to one-eighth of the sales charge, or from 1 to 2.5 percent of the purchase price on smaller purchases, with the balance (6 to 7.5 percent) going to the retailer. Some principal underwriters are general securities firms and expect to handle all the fund's security purchases and sales themselves. They frequently must turn over a larger portion of the total charge in the underwriting to other retailers to make up for the fact that the latter will not get "reciprocal business" when the fund begins to operate. One such underwriter pays dealers 7.5 percent of a total 8 percent load.

The portion of the sales charge kept by the main underwriter is intended to cover overhead and general administrative expenses, most of the cost of prospectuses, the cost of sales literature supplied to retailers, and other promotional and advertising expenses. Promotional expenses may include compensation paid to field representatives or to wholesalers of the underwriter.

The 6 to 7.5 percent received by the retail dealer is shared with the individual salespeople, generally on a straight commission basis, and with supervisory personnel who may make a commission on the sales of the salespeople they supervise. The dealer himself generally realizes compensation ranging from 1.5 to 4.5 percent of the total purchase price.

The prospectus also describes the fees that the investment adviser will get for his services and the nature of those services as well. All material arrangements between the fund and its adviser must be clearly described.

The SEC requires a fund to reveal all unfavorable material facts about itself in its prospectus — such potentially damaging information as, for example, the facts concerning prior disciplinary or criminal proceedings against fund officers.

The laws requiring such "full disclosure" can bite hard. After a registration has become effective, if it is discovered that the prospectus lies about or fails to disclose an important detail and that the public therefore could have been misled, the boom can be lowered on everyone responsible — directors and officers of the fund who signed the prospectus, accountants who put their stamp on the financial statements, underwriters, and even appraisers whose faulty opinions might have led the public to buy the shares. Shareholders may sue to get their money back.

You Too Can Manage a Portfolio

According to the law, anyone can manage a mutual fund portfolio. The investment adviser is only a firm that holds the lucrative contract, and it may hold nothing more. It may subcontract out the work of analyzing stocks. If so, it generally pays subcontractors much lower fees than it itself obtains. Indeed, it may choose whomever it wishes to manage a portfolio.

Nobody agrees on the qualifications necessary in a good portfolio manager. For appearance's sake, if nothing else, many advisory firms want their portfolio managers to hold advanced degrees. They theorize that a wretched performance by a Ph.D. in economics hurts less than a similar bomb-out by their former office clerk. Theoretically, a graduate of the Harvard Business School with ten years' apprenticeship in security analysis should possess a superior ability to dig into the financial condition and prospects of a corporation and should have a greater comprehension of the hazards of the marketplace. In practice, many analysts believe that a "sixth sense," "intuition," or "gut reactions" are more important.

According to the SEC study of institutional investors, the management of the advisory firm in small funds is, in effect, the portfolio manager. In larger fund complexes decision-making generally is more decentralized. In the largest companies an investment committee of the senior management usually generates an approved list of securities or general investment policy. The portfolio managers, with authority ranging from complete to limited, implement policies for their funds. On the average, fund complexes have approximately 5.8 portfolio managers per firm.

In large fund complexes portfolio managers spend about 75 percent of their time in investment decision-making and supervision of portfolios. The percentages are smaller for small fund organizations, where portfolio managers have a broader range of duties. Typical fund analysts spend 34 percent of their time in contact with portfolio companies.

The fundamental approach (where emphasis is on analysis

and projections of corporate earnings) is the most important to the average fund advisory firm. Seventy-seven percent of the total sample said that this approach was always used. Technical approaches appear only of moderate interest; sixty-three percent of the total sample said that this approach was not used frequently.

Ostensibly, the most important sources of external information for fund decision-makers are the financial statements of issuers of securities. Such statements include annual reports, prospectuses, and proxy statements issued when important corporate changes are submitted to stockholders for a vote. Direct contact with security issuers ranks next, followed by information received from other research organizations and, finally, information purchased from broker-dealers via commission dollars. Information from other investment advisers on a contractual basis appears to be relatively unimportant for most firms.[13]

Are Fund Advisers Overpaid?

At first glance, application of a mechanical formula for compensating fund advisers seems eminently reasonable. The adviser increases the fund's assets; why shouldn't the adviser benefit appropriately? The assumption is that assets grow because of the adviser's wise investment decisions. This happens, of course. But assets also grow when the fund sells more shares. Thus the mediocre adviser who has done poorly for fund shareholders may owe his or her increased income solely to the fund's effective selling mechanism.

Advisers have found that their incomes rise more through their salespeople's efforts than through their ability to make profits for shareholders in the stock market. Hence they compete vigorously to encourage salespeople to push the fund's shares more strongly.

Fund managers have been able to maintain advisory fees at a general level of .5 percent because they can show that, as a manager testified at a Senate hearing, "This fee amounts to peanuts for the average investor." On your $5,000 investment in a fund, for example, you pay the adviser only $25 a year.

The SEC does not buy this argument. In a lengthy position paper issued in 1967, it countered:

Even the most outrageously exorbitant fees or charges can be made to seem "reasonable" if their impact is divided among a sufficiently large group. Would it be unreasonable on this basis, for instance, for each American to pay the President of the United States one penny per year for his efforts in administering our country's affairs? Based on a population of 200 million, this would amount to $2 million a year. Would it be unreasonable for each American to contribute a nickel ($10 million a year) or a dime ($20 million a year)? The industry cannot detract from the significance of advisory fee rates by resorting to the device of allocating the $140,000,000 collected as advisory fees among several million investors. The division of the total advisory fees levied on investors in mutual funds in minute fragments does not in any way affect the judgment that they are too high.[14]

Fund critics also argue that the cumulative effect of advisory fees on the individual shareholder's investment may in the long run be substantial. The difference between .5 and .25 percent would amount to more than 5 percent over a 20-year span. The investor also must sustain the burden of other significant expenses, such as the cost of portfolio turnover, the annual rate of which is substantially higher for funds than for other institutions and the market as a whole.

A 1967 SEC report revealed that mutual fund advisory fees per dollar of assets managed substantially exceed those charged by banks to manage pension and profit-sharing plans. Of course, the latter are in a position to negotiate effectively the charges they pay; unlike most mutual funds, trustees of these plans select the adviser themselves. With competitive forces at work, therefore, economies of scale are passed on to their clients.

Typical advisory fee schedules published by banks for investment management service to pension and profit-sharing plans call for a fee of .06 percent of total asset value for a pension or profit-sharing plan portfolio of $100 million — one-eighth of the typical advisory fee paid by mutual funds of comparable size. Moreover, some pension funds or profit-sharing plans may be able to negotiate further savings. And mutual funds organized as vehicles for equity investment for banks, members of professional groups, and employee groups pay management fees that follow a similar pattern. In some cases the fee is as low as

one-tenth of 1 percent of the first $10 million of assets, with
lower fee rates for higher asset levels.

The SEC has commented:

> We do not suggest that mutual fund advisory fee rates should
> be the same as fees for pensions and profit-sharing plans. Since
> the services required by the two investment media and the
> indirect benefits received by banks and advisers from their manage-
> ment functions are not precisely the same, some difference in the
> fee rates charged to mutual funds and to pension and profit-
> sharing plans at any given size level may be justifiable. But
> neither this difference in function, which exists principally in the
> area of management services provided rather than the area of
> investment advice, nor the fact that such services, frequently
> only ministerial, are provided, nor any possible difference in
> performance can justify the existing patterns of charges levied
> on investment companies.
>
> As industry representatives have noted, the fees charged by
> banks and other investment advisers to individual clients on
> relatively small amounts of assets are often as high or higher than
> those charged to investment companies, but as the size of the
> assets managed grows, even when the amounts by comparison
> with investment companies are relatively modest, the fees scale
> down sharply. The same investment advisers that charge their
> multimillion dollar fund clients advisory fees in the neighborhood
> of 0.50 percent often charge their nonfund clients with portfolios
> of only $1 million to $2 million — relatively insignificant when
> compared with the assets of the typical large funds — substantially
> less, and fees on larger nonfund portfolios are subject to negotia-
> tion of even lower rates. We have found no evidence of higher
> costs which might provide some justification for the substantially
> higher management remuneration obtained from fund clients.[15]

As Manuel Cohen told a House committee hearing:

> The problems of mutual fund acquisition and management
> costs cannot be dismissed because many mutual fund shareholders
> have profited substantially from their fund investments during
> the rapidly rising equity markets in the past two decades. Nowhere
> in the securities markets have charges for transactions been
> justified by the ultimate profitability of the investment, and we do
> not believe that charges for the acquisition of mutual fund shares
> can be justified on this basis.[16]

Mutual fund managers like to take the credit for increases in assets per share. But appreciation of fund shares occurred almost automatically when the market as a whole was going up. Almost anybody could make money under such conditions. The following statement was made during a 1967 congressional hearing:

> Many other investors who participated in the rising equity markets of recent years without the benefit of the portfolio diversification and professional management offered by mutual funds have tended to fare well. Studies by various scholars in this field have compared mutual fund performance of randomly selected portfolios of securities which have remained unchanged for the entire periods studied. These studies have shown that on the average, and it is important to stress the term "average," these portfolios have done better than the average mutual fund.[17]

Defenders of the mutual fund industry refer to their sales and management fees as "bargain basement costs" for individual investors. The SEC, however, has maintained:

> The combination of sales charges, advisory fees, and brokerage commissions which an investor must pay in connection with his mutual fund investment represents the most expensive way ever devised by the securities industry for mass participation in the securities market. Mutual fund costs are no more "bargain basement" than the quality of their product. Although mutual funds offer a security of high quality, the high cost of a mutual fund investment places investors at a substantial disadvantage in the achievement of their financial goals.
>
> Justification of advisory fees in terms of the cost to the individual investor is inconsistent with the basic concept of a mutual fund. Mutual funds are created and sold to the public as a "mutual" investment medium through the pooling of individual savings for investment in equity securities just as mutual savings banks offer a way to pool savings for investment in home mortgages and other debt securities and mutual insurance companies offer a way to pool premiums and thus reduce costs of family protection.
>
> While the industry has created the funds and sold their shares with all the trappings and attractions of "mutual" savings institutions, its representatives attempt to suggest that the externally managed fund is not a mutual savings institution at all, but more

comparable to a stock insurance company. But neither stock insurance companies nor a major segment of any other industry are characterized by the externally-managed structure, which compensates its managers not on the value of their services but on the value of the company's assets. Such a method of compensation, which expresses the compensation as a fraction of one percent of the fund, only obscures the many millions of dollars in managerial emoluments that flow from control of a mutual fund. The industry cannot have it both ways, selling shares in a mutual savings institution while abandoning any attempt to operate the institution for the mutual benefit of its investors.

Indeed, even in the ordinary corporate situation, where no attempt is made to create a corporate entity with the trappings of mutuality, the propriety of self-dealing transactions, such as management compensation, is not measured in terms of the cost per shareholders or cost per customer. When a director of a manufacturing company causes his company to deal with a supplier in which he has a financial interest and the supplier overcharges the company, the transaction has never been thought to be justified on the grounds that it costs each shareholder only a few cents. Such a transaction is condemned as a breach of fiduciary duty because it contravenes the norms of the business community and the basic tradition of the law.[18]

Additional evidence of gross overcompensation of fund advisers is suggested by the fact that "internally managed" funds — those that hire investment advisers as employees — pay substantially less for their investment advice than do "externally managed" companies, which are set up by the advisers who have organized the funds. During the fiscal years ending in 1966 of 11 such companies, cost ratios ranged from .12 percent to .40 percent of average net assets. The median management cost ratio was .24 percent — one-half the median advisory fee rate for 59 externally managed funds of the same size. Advisory fees of funds with external managers ranged from .24 percent to .66 percent of average net assets.

However, internal managers are still richly rewarded. Massachusetts Investors Growth Stock Fund, for example, had a management cost ratio of only .26 percent, and an affiliated fund, Massachusetts Investors Trust, had a ratio of only .13

percent, one of the smallest of all the funds in the country. Yet these funds paid five trustee-directors a total of $2,223,093 in 1966, an average of almost $450,000 each. Two other directors received $241,457 each.

The Incentive Fee Problem

Until recently many funds had incentive fee arrangements whereby their advisers received bonuses if the fund outperformed a major market index. But the advisers continued to receive their normal fees and were not penalized if the fund did worse than the average. As a result of vociferous public criticism, however, this practice has been generally discontinued. Funds that pay extra for good performance are expected to exact penalties for a poor showing.

A typical arrangement is that of the Burnham Fund, which pays the usual advisory fee of .5 percent of the average net asset value during any year. If the fund's performance exceeds that of Standard and Poor's index of 500 stocks, its adviser may receive additional fees of up to 3.5 percent of the fund's net asset value. If the investment performance of the index in any year exceeds that of the fund, a negative adjustment may be applied to reduce or eliminate incentive fees previously earned but not yet paid. However, the adviser receives the base fee no matter how poorly the fund performs.

According to Hamer Budge, former chairman of the SEC, arrangements such as these are still unfair. The fund pays the adviser fees for favorable performance as they are earned. However, any credit the adviser owes the fund due to fund underperformance is seldom repaid. Instead, it is used as an offset against future fees. Where future fees are not adequate to absorb the offset, the debt is often simply forgotten.

But, demands Budge, if the fund must pay fees to the adviser immediately for performance, why should amounts owed by the adviser be deferred and the fund be deprived of a return on the amounts owed to it? Further, these arrangements provide no assurance that advisers are financially able to meet their future obligations. According to the law, each advisory contract may be terminated by the fund on 60 days' notice. It would be only prudent to have advisers who have the financial ability to pay promptly any amounts owed to the funds in the event their contracts are terminated.

Some incentive fee arrangements are so complicated that hardly anyone can understand them. In testimony before a House subcommittee on Commerce and Finance, Budge introduced excerpts from the prospectuses of the Hartwell and Campbell Leverage and Gibraltar Growth funds that his staff found very confusing. For example, the Gibraltar "explanation" read:

> For its services as Investment Adviser, the Fund pays Gibraltar Research and Management Company a quarterly fee of one-eighth of 1% (equivalent to ½ of 1% per annum) of the average net asset value of the fund. In addition, the Fund pays the Investment Adviser, annually, 10% of (1) the Fund's net realized gains from sales of securities, reduced by any net unrealized depreciation in the Fund's portfolio during the year (being a difference between unrealized gains and unrealized losses), and (2) dividends and interest received or receivable by the Fund during [the] year. In the event that an unrealized net loss is taken into account for the purpose of computing, the management feel the value of the securities used at the end of the year for the purpose of computing such net loss shall be taken as the cost of such securities in computing future management fees to the extent that such unrealized losses have been used in the actual reduction of realized gains. Provided, however, that no additional management fee shall be payable unless all realized and unrealized capital gains less realized and unrealized capital losses from the inception of the Fund, plus all dividends and interest received from the inception of the Fund, plus all interest and dividends then receivable are at least 10 times all management fees previously paid and then proposed to be paid. Regardless of the amount of net realized profit in any one year, the total management fee for any year shall in no case be greater than the cumulative total of 4% of year-end net 2½% of the average net asset value during the year, even though the net asset value of the Fund decreased during the year. However, the incentive adjustment of 2% of average net asset value cannot be paid for a year in which the Fund shares declined in value (after allowance for the capital gains distribution) and must be carried forward for payment out of an increase in value in a subsequent year. The .5% fee and the incentive adjustment will be accrued daily and taken into account in

computing the net asset value of a fund share for the purposes of determining the redemption price, and offering price, if any, per share, but the incentive adjustment for the current year will not be accrued for the purpose of calculating the incentive adjustment for that year.

When SEC staff members inquired of counsel as to the meaning of the prospectus, the counsel of the Gibraltar Fund said that he could not figure out the meaning either. He referred the matter to the fund's accountant. The latter admitted he could not understand the provisions at first sight, but he indicated that he would be able to do so if permitted to give them further consideration and to discuss them with the fund's controller. Similarly, the counsel for the Hartwell and Campbell Fund said that he understood the fee arrangements but added that a "very detailed analysis" was necessary to understand them.[19]

The Reciprocity Problem

The roots of the problem of reciprocity ("You [brokers] sell my fund and I'll give you the business of buying and selling shares for me") are deep. A 1962 study by the Wharton School of Finance and Commerce found: "The sale of mutual fund shares by broker-dealers is the most important factor affecting the brokerage allocations of the numerous open-end company groups selling their shares in volume through independent dealers." In its 1966 report on mutual funds, the SEC also found:

> The managers of most dealer-distributed funds which are not closely affiliated with brokerage houses use a substantial portion of the funds' brokerage to pay dealers extra compensation for sales of fund shares. The amount of brokerage available for sales depends upon a variety of factors, but generally the larger funds and fund complexes are able to use a much greater percentage of their brokerage for sales than are the smaller ones.

The Federal Trade Commission has said that reciprocity transforms substantial buying power into a weapon for "denying competitors less favorably situated access to the market." It

distorts the focus of the trader by interposing between the
trader and the traditional competitive factors of price, quality,
and service an irrelevant and alien factor that destroys fair and
free competition based on merit. The efficient producer may
thereby suffer loss because of a circumstance extrinsic to the
worth of his product.

Additional complications in the securities industry arise
from the fact that reciprocal practices create the conflicts
regarding the fiduciary relationship between the money manager and his beneficiary. Thus has the SEC directed attention
to potential problems of reciprocal arrangements at the fund
management level:

> The increasing importance of brokerage as compensation for
> sales of fund shares presents a potential for harmful effects on
> fund management. The need to allocate brokerage for sales may
> tempt fund advisers to skimp on the allocation of brokerage for
> investment advice or other nonsales services of greater benefit to
> the funds than the accelerated sales of new shares. Even more
> important, it creates pressures for "churning," i.e., frequent sales
> and purchases of portfolio securities unwarranted by investment
> considerations for the purpose of generating brokerage com-
> missions. It can lead fund managers to eschew those markets
> where the best prices in portfolio transactions might have been
> obtained and may cause them to pay unnecessary charges for the
> execution of such transactions. Thus, mutual funds have made
> appreciably less use than other institutional investors of the
> third market, which has no minimum commission schedule and
> therefore cannot provide give-ups.

The commission also found potential dangers at the broker-
dealer level:

> Mutual fund reciprocal and give-up practices also may impair
> the integrity of dealer recommendations upon which customers
> rely. They operate as hidden influences by tempting dealers to
> base their recommendations on the amount of brokerage and
> give-ups received rather than on the investment needs of their
> customers. . . . It places small funds and fund complexes, which
> cannot allocate as much brokerage for sales as larger ones, at a
> distinct disadvantage in competing for dealer favor.[20]

Figures from the SEC debunk the notion that superiority of research distinguishes brokerage firms that obtain the funds' buy and sell orders from brokerage firms that get none. These figures show that in 1968 all NYSE firms had research expenses of $97 million, a mere 2.4 percent of their total expenses. Of course, firms dealing primarily with institutional investors spent more on research than did firms dealing mainly with the public. But the median expense for "institutional firms" was only $129,000 a year — the cost of one junior analyst, two senior analysts, and their secretaries. In contrast, median research expense per retail firm was $45,000. These figures suggest that the retail firms realize that even an additional $100,000 a year expended on research would not be sufficient to get some lucrative commission business.[21]

It is perhaps natural that the total brokerage fees paid by funds affiliated with brokerage houses tend to be on the high side. For example, the rate of portfolio turnover for the Guardian Fund, a no-load trust sponsored by the New York Exchange brokerage firm of Neuberger and Berman, for the fiscal years ending October 31, 1968, 1969, and 1970, were 81.5, 73.1, and 107.2 percent, respectively. These amounts were well above average. This is a relatively small fund; its total assets in 1970 were only $46 million. Nevertheless, during these three years it paid brokerage commissions to Neuberger and Berman of $419,013, $302,685, and $431,062, respectively. During the 1970 fiscal year the fund paid total brokerage commissions of $529,493 — more than 1 percent of its assets. In addition, it paid $8,988 to Rosenthal and Company and $9,380 to Glickenhaus and Company, brokerage houses that were represented on its board of directors.

Not all funds managed by brokerage houses give their commission business to those houses. For example, the company managing the Chemical Fund is owned by the New York Stock Exchange member firm of F. Eberstadt and Company but has a policy of placing its portfolio business elsewhere to avoid conflict-of-interest charges. Not surprisingly, this fund's portfolio turnover rate in 1968, 1969, and 1970 was 5.2, 10.3, and 12.1 percent, respectively — less than one-fifth the industry average.

In the past, mutual funds often directed stock exchange firms executing orders to "give up" part of their commissions to other broker-dealers whom the funds desired to reward for selling large quantities of their shares. Critics argued that "customer directed give-ups" were equivalent to "rebating" part of the commission except that the rebate did not benefit the fund. Sometimes a brokerage firm allied to the fund received the added commissions. To remedy this situation all registered national securities exchanges adopted rules prohibiting customer-directed give-ups, on December 5, 1968.

The Light at the End of the Tunnel?

Many securities industry observers strongly believe that the SEC has failed as a watchdog of the funds. They believe that existing abuses would not be possible if the SEC exercised its full powers on behalf of fund investors. Whether such criticisms are valid or not, the SEC in recent years has taken a sterner look at fund operations and has adopted measures that inspire hopes of a somewhat better break for investors. Recent legal cases also suggest that the docile fund investor who compulsorily accepted managements' decisions may be a figure of the past.

In 1970 Congress passed and President Nixon signed the Investment Company Amendments Act. This act was designed to provide greater protection for fund shareholders, though it did not provide the full added protection sought by the SEC. Under this act, investment advisers for funds were charged with a specific fiduciary duty, and a breach of this duty will enable the SEC or shareholders to sue on the grounds that the management fee was excessive.

An SEC survey showed that of the 137 registered investment companies with performance fee arrangements as of June 30, 1969, 48 arrangements provided no penalty to the adviser for poor performance (although they provided for significant incentive rewards), and another 45 arrangements that provided for a penalty were structured so that the potential rewards were substantially greater than the possible penalty. "The inequity in the fee structures of those 93 companies is patently clear," the survey report stated. "It is a one-way street in favor of the adviser. With little or no penalty for poor performance, the adviser has everything to gain and little or nothing to lose in striving for maximum short-term performance, regardless of the risks involved."[22] One can hope that this "Heads I win, tails you lose" practice has reached its end.

In 1972 the SEC announced that it was prepared to stop the long-established practice by which funds give their brokerage business to brokers who do the best job of selling their shares. The SEC said that it would ask the National Association of Security Dealers to instruct its members, including numerous institutional investors, to discontinue this "reciprocity." The SEC has also publicly discussed adopting rules to prevent the practice should the NASD fail to act. Wall Street cynics have doubted, however, that such a prohibition can be enforced. "Funds must give their brokerage business to someone," a veteran analyst observed. "Who will they give it to — somebody who does nothing for them?"

In 1972 the SEC also announced that it would lower to $300,000 the value of brokerage orders above which brokers would have to negotiate their commissions with their customers rather than use the standard commission rate. In theory, such negotiated commissions result in lower fees on large orders and consequently reduce mutual fund expenditures.

In the same year the SEC said that it would not object to a membership on a national stock exchange for a brokerage firm affiliated with one or several mutual funds, provided the "predominant" part of its brokerage business comes from unaffiliated investors. "Predominant," as defined by the SEC, was to signify more than half, but a precise definition was not immediately forthcoming.

Funds have held seats on regional exchanges such as the Pacific Coast Exchange and the Philadelphia-Baltimore-Washington Exchange, but both the New York and American Stock Exchanges forbade membership for brokers considered to be "captives" of the mutual funds. (Broker-members of such exchanges were permitted to own and operate mutual funds, and some have profited handsomely.)

The Investors Diversified Services, the nation's largest mutual fund organization, with assets of more than $7 billion and its own sales organization, sought in 1971 to buy a seat on the New

York Exchange for Jefferies and Company, its brokerage subsidiary. The huge brokerage business it generates and the fact that it does not need brokers to sell its shares to the public left IDS in an ideal position to profit from an exchange membership. However, the Jefferies's application was turned down. To justify this NYSE President Robert W. Haack cited Rule 318, which states that a member firm must have brokerage as its "primary purpose" and must derive at least 50 percent of its gross income from broker-dealer operations. IDS itself might qualify under this clause, inasmuch as it is registered with the SEC as a broker-dealer. But IDS also has a parent. It is a subsidiary of the Allegheny Corporation, a holding company that plainly does not qualify.

This rejection did not end the efforts of big fund complexes to secure their own seats on exchanges, and they proceeded to test the exchange's membership policies under the antitrust laws. Some benefit to fund shareholders could result from a successful court battle if funds are permitted to pocket the commissions that now go to outsiders. Cynics would not bet on it, however, for many brokerage firms operate mutual funds themselves and use them to produce commissions. Moreover, portfolio turnover rates of some of these funds suggest that their managers will find ways to profit from in-house brokerage at the expense of fund shareholders whenever possible.

Another much needed regulation may limit the rights of fund management companies to sell themselves to the highest bidder without regard for the shareholders. There is great potential for harm in the fact that mutual fund management organizations are considered salable properties because of their fund commission contracts. A growing traffic developed: original founders, eager for capital gains, sought potential buyers among insurance companies, brokerage firms, and other financial houses eager for heady profits. Such trafficking, however, could seriously harm the shareholders.

Of course, a fund's ability to do a good job for its shareholders depends upon its advisers. Those who make the buy or sell decisions for the fund are entirely responsible for its profits or losses. Once the advisory contract becomes a piece of merchandise to be bought and sold, however, shareholders' interests began to be neglected. When selling its control of the fund, a management organization naturally would favor the highest bidder. *Whether this bidder would do a good job for the fund's shareholders need not be considered at all.* As a practical matter, shareholders demonstrated no real power to veto such a sale. The principal of one management organization that merged into another candidly admitted why this particular partner was chosen: "They offered the best price. This was our consideration. No one else offered that, or even close to it."[23]

Several successful legal actions in recent years, however, inspire hopes that shareholders will receive more equitable treatment in the future.

For example, in a development of potentially great significance, in 1972 a federal court judge approved a proposed settlement of a shareholders' suit arising from the sale of the Lazard Fund five years earlier. The Lazard Fund, owned by Lazard Freres and Company, was sold to Dun and Bradstreet for $2.5 million worth of shares in the latter corporation. (The fund is now known as Moody's Capital Fund.) After protracted litigation Lazard agreed to settle the claim for $1 million, thus implicitly recognizing the long-neglected rights of shareholders.

In another promising case charges were leveled that the Lehman Brothers brokerage firm had improperly executed portfolio transactions for the Lehman Corporation, a closed-end investment company that it sponsors. This case began in 1965 when the stockholders, represented by the law firm headed by Abraham L. Pomerantz, alleged that Lehman Brothers had interposed itself between the fund and dealers in the over-the-counter market. The suit alleged that not being permitted to buy and sell through over-the-counter dealers directly, the fund was forced to pay extra commissions to the sponsoring company. The suit also charged that the fund's expenses were increased when Lehman Brothers failed to execute its buy and sell orders in the most economical way. Specifically, the suit alleged, large stockholders often can use the "third market" — that is, negotiate purchases and sales between themselves — to avoid the brokerage fees involved in trading on a stock exchange. By failing to use the third market in many transactions, the suit charged, Lehman caused the fund to pay more for portfolio transactions than necessary. After six years of litigation the defendant agreed to settle the suit out of court by paying $250,000 to the investment company, paying up to $40,000 of the plaintiff's legal fees, agreeing to interpose no more, and agreeing to provide proof that future over-the-counter transactions handled by Lehman Brothers for the fund would cost no more than if they were handled in any other way.[24]

In another precedent-setting decision a federal appeals court in Boston found the management firm of the Fidelity group of mutual funds guilty of "gross misconduct" for failing to obtain refunds on commissions of certain brokerage fees paid by one or several of its funds. The Fidelity group is one of the most prestigious in the fund industry. The president of its management firm — the Fidelity Management and Research Company — is Edward C. Johnson II, whom some financial writers have called "Mr. Mutual Fund" himself.

5

Funds Are Born to Be Sold

Theoretically, the fact that the adviser's fee
grows simultaneously with the fund's assets encourages him to
increase assets by increasing the value of each share. However,
total assets can be increased even faster by increasing the
amounts shareholders invest in the fund. For example, Ben
Brilliant, ambitious organizer of the Brilliant Fund, considers
his options. He knows — even if his shareholders do not — that
substantially increasing the value of each share is a long, often
wearisome process. More dramatic results and larger fees can
be achieved by an aggressive sales program to bring new
money into the fund. But if he wants to get independent
salespeople to sell his fund instead of another, he must offer
special inducements: higher sales commissions on the fund
sales themselves, perhaps coupled with additional commissions
for handling the fund's own buy and sell transactions.

For most funds, selling shares to the public is the whole
game. "It's probably fair to say that most shares in a mutual

fund aren't bought; they're sold — and sold by some pretty high-pressure, high-cost methods," Louis Engel wrote in *How to Buy Stocks*.[1] Millions of paperback copies of this book were distributed by Merrill Lynch, Pierce, Fenner and Smith during the period in which it refused to handle mutual funds. (This refusal, as already indicated, was based on the conviction that better results for the small investor could be achieved with its own investment suggestions.) Now Merrill Lynch is in the fund business itself. Nevertheless, the original indictment stands: when a large sales commission is involved, fund shares are *sold*; when the customer does the investigating himself and selects a no-load fund, fund shares are *bought*. The ratio of load shares to no-load shares outstanding, currently about ten to one, suggests the extent to which fund shares are sold and not bought. As one fund manager has commented, "Funds are born to be sold." And, he might have added, fund organizers unprepared to do aggressive selling would do better to leave their funds unborn.

That most mutual funds are sold rather than bought is borne out by the fate of stocks of closed-end investment companies and dual-purpose funds.

Closed-end investment companies resemble mutual funds in their investment objectives. However, their managements do not redeem shares at the prevailing net asset value. Shares in a closed-end company must be sold through a broker, precisely as shares in General Motors or IBM are sold. The prices of these shares are thus subject to the vagaries of the marketplace and the whim of investors. For the most part, except at the peak of a long bull market, prices bid for closed-end companies are substantially below what the shares would be worth if the company sold its assets and divided the proceeds. At the end of 1970, 18 of the 24 leading closed-end funds could be bought at prices below their asset value. A few discounts were really remarkable. Diebold Venture Capital Fund, for example, listed assets of $11.12 per share, but its stock was offered at $5.75. Twelve dollars and eighty-five cents of assets in the SMC Investment Company could be purchased for $7.

In dual-purpose funds, a British creation, income flows in one of two directions. Dividend and interest income goes to income shares, while appreciation in asset value is credited to capital shares. As of the end of 1970, capital shares of four of the seven largest dual-purpose funds sold at prices substantially below asset value; two sold at slight premiums. Gerald Tsai's Hemisphere Fund sold at a premium of 89 percent but only because its net assets had dropped so low — from $10 to $1.72 — that huge tax benefits could accrue if its losses were later offset by capital gains.

Many analysts believe that closed-end and dual-purpose shares available at a discount are better values than mutual fund shares: the investor gets more assets for his money. But since the securities salesperson earns only ordinary commissions in selling them, it is more profitable to push mutual funds. The buyer of closed-end and dual-purpose shares must often act on his own initiative. As a rule, the "bargain" nature of these companies reflects investor neglect.

Curiously, despite their tradition of being sold at a discount, new issues of closed-end funds are not difficult to place with the public. Perhaps the reason for this is the underwriters' greater commissions on new stock offerings than on shares already outstanding. As soon as aggressive salespitches are discontinued, such shares generally drop to a price commensurate with their underlying assets.

Selling Load Funds

"Load" funds generally are sold in one of three ways: (1) by salespeople directly employed by the fund organization; (2) by salespeople working for registered investment dealers who usually sell only funds; (3) by brokerage house salespeople ("account executives" or "registered representatives") who sell fund shares in addition to stocks, bonds, commodities, and other investment vehicles. Each of these sales methods poses definite hazards for the individual investor.

The salespeople directly employed by the fund management company obviously owe total allegiance to their employer. Usually they are limited to selling a half-dozen funds with different investment objectives — that is, all the funds that their employer manages. Some companies permit their salespeople to sell other funds, but they pay a lower commission on such sales than they pay for selling their own funds. This means, of course, that the salespeople will try to sell one of their firm's funds regardless of its record. Generally, funds with "captive" sales organizations are the largest in the field. But by and large their performance records have been quite mediocre.

In dealing with such salespeople you are unlikely to get anything resembling the impartial investment advice for which you will be asked to pay a hefty sales commission.

The typical brokerage house salesperson concentrates on relatively few funds. He is apt to sell those that bring the greatest personal benefit; whether they benefit the customers is not the salesperson's primary consideration. For example, an employer may be underwriting a new fund and may offer the salesperson a higher commission than usual to spur sales. The firm may also "specialize" in dealing with certain types of funds — funds that offer commission business to firms as a reward for selling their shares.

The fact that mutual funds pay a sales charge to buy or sell stocks produces many cozy relationships: the broker sells the fund's shares and, in addition to the full commission on those sales, is also rewarded with some or all of the fund's brokerage business. Such an arrangement may tempt the salesperson to ignore the fact that the fund being sold is inappropriate for the client. When personal interest conflicts with that of the customer, private interest usually prevails. A wider choice of funds is offered by salespeople for investment firms that sell mutual funds exclusively, but this selection is by no means exhaustive. Nevertheless, an experienced fund salesperson of this type can provide competent advice well worth the price you pay for it.

Theoretically, a fund dealer may sell shares in any fund. In practice, the dealer may concentrate his efforts on no more than a dozen — that is, those that have been sold successfully in the past, those the dealer knows something about, those that may give the dealer special favors such as kickbacks in the form of orders for shares bought or sold in the over-the-counter market.

The dealer is likely to be influenced by the nature of the sales promotion made by a fund. Because of this, funds without their own sales organizations frequently employ "wholesalers" to promote their product to dealers and fund salespeople. These promotion people employ all of the persuasive arts to convince retailers of the quality of their product.

Of course, fund dealers often push "hot" funds — those with meteoric, though perhaps erratic, investment records. For example, it was easy in 1967 to sell shares in an Enterprise Fund when every newspaper in the country lauded its double-your-money-in-a-year performance. Fund dealers did not discuss "no-load" funds regardless of their suitability.

Some fund dealers conscientiously try to fit the investor to a fund that fits him or her. But here too the possibility exists that the independent salesperson or dealer will try to push off on you those funds that are more advantageous to sell.

J. A. Livingston, financial editor of the *Philadelphia Bulletin*, accurately summed up the problem before a congressional committee hearing in 1967: Mutual fund salespeople are subject to a double pull — their self-interest against the interest of the investor, often a person unskilled in finance or economics. This conflict is inherent in the stocks-and-bonds business. Wall Street manufactures securities for sale. A securities salesperson has the job of persuading investors to buy the merchandise that is for sale. Yet at the same time, the salesperson tries to advise investors on what is best for them. Thus the agent wears two hats — the hat of the salesperson anxious to earn a commission and the hat of the investment counselor or adviser, duty-bound to help clients and customers. When the showdown comes, who is served?[2]

Fund organizations frequently run sales contests with inducements such as cash, automobiles, and all-expense-paid trips to such places as Miami, Bermuda, and the French Riviera for the salespeople who sell the greatest number of fund shares. Will a salesperson who can receive a Camaro sports coupe by dint of selling you one fund instead of another restrain himself or herself simply because this fund may be less suitable for you?

What It Takes to Become a Fund Salesperson

The qualifications required to become a mutual fund salesperson are minimal. The prospective fund salesperson needs only to prove that he or she has a record free of serious crime, and that he or she possesses sufficient knowledge to pass a test administered by the National Association of Securities Dealers. It should be noted that this test is so simple that people with no previous knowledge of investing pass it after a few days of intensive study. Some mutual fund organizations conduct more intensive training courses for their salespeople. Assuredly these courses are primarily designed to teach them how to make sales, not to understand the complexities of fund investing. Even less are salespeople taught to select from the hundreds of funds available that which best suits a particular customer. At best, the salesperson is taught to choose the most suitable fund from the half dozen or so that the employer handles. The salesperson will guide you to the fund that promises the most satisfactory performance for you in the same way that a Chevrolet dealer will sell you the Chevrolet that best suits your purpose. If a Cadillac or a jeep would serve you better, you are out of luck.

In common with almost everyone else in the investment business, mutual fund salespeople claim special knowledge and expertise that other mortals can ignore only at great peril. They know that the average person lacks the intelligence to choose a suitable fund independently.

A critical (though accurate) picture of the qualifications many fund salespeople bring to their task was portrayed by SEC Chairman Manuel Cohen in a statement to the House Committee on Interstate and Foreign Commerce on October 24, 1967. Cohen declared:

> Selling mutual funds is an easy occupation to enter. Almost anyone not found guilty of a serious crime can become a mutual fund salesman. And since fund salesmen are, with rare exceptions, compensated on a pure commission basis, another salesman adds little to the employer's costs. Any sales that the new salesman makes (no matter how few or small) produce income for the employer. It is a case of the more the merrier. There is a typical pattern. Each new salesman makes — or tries to make — sales to his friends and relatives. Carrying his selling efforts beyond that is more difficult. Prospects aren't that numerous because the ratio of salesmen to prospective investors is so high. Mr. Cornelius

Roach of Waddell & Reed, Inc., estimated before this Committee that there are about 90,000 people selling mutual funds. Since there are approximately 4 million mutual fund shareholders, there is, by Mr. Roach's estimate, a mutual fund salesman for every 44 existing mutual fund shareholders. Even if one were to estimate that there are only 50,000 mutual fund salesmen, there would be a mutual fund salesman for every 80 mutual fund investors. So it is inevitable that many full-time salesmen find it very hard to earn a good livelihood solely from the sale of fund shares. When a salesman does manage to unearth somebody who could invest in a mutual fund, he often finds that one of the army of part-time salesmen or a full-time salesman from a large New York Stock Exchange firm has already made the sale. Hence the turnover rate among salesmen is very high.

In few other areas of the American economy does the labor force rotate at a comparable rate. New recruits who believe — or who are led to believe — that selling mutual funds is an open road to riches, or at least a dignified way in which to add a meaningful supplement to an income primarily derived from some other source, are offset by equal numbers of dropouts who have found that it isn't quite as easy to make money selling mutual funds as the recruiter said it was.

Just as it is relatively easy to become a mutual fund salesman, it is not difficult to become a mutual fund dealer. All it takes is $2,500, which can be borrowed. Many salesmen who tire of sharing what they produce with their employers venture into business for themselves. But the same obstacles that the proprietors of these new mutual fund retailing firms faced as salesmen still confront them and their sales recruits. Hence the high entry rate among mutual fund dealers is counterbalanced by a high departure rate.[3]

Whatever training the new recruit receives is sales training with one overriding objective: to get merchandise into your hands.

In most large funds the sales divisions operate their own training programs. For two weeks or so, they give the neophyte a two-part course: part one consists of discussions by supervisors or regular instructors to help the student pass NASD and state examinations so that the applicant may be registered as a fund salesperson; the second part consists of selling techniques. To pass the examinations the applicant must know something about the nature of mutual funds and the securities business, the basic rules covering the sale of fund shares, and a bit about federal and state securities and tax laws.

Phase two of the course is designed to make the sales recruit believe that mutual funds are inevitable for everybody and to show the recruit not only how to locate prospective clients but how to get their signatures on the dotted line. In addition, the recruit is informed of the kinds of claims and practices considered *verboten* under the securities laws.

Defenders of the fund industry claim that this basically minimal training program is not over when the salesperson completes the course. Instruction, they assert, is a continuing process, carried on through publications, sales meetings, and seminars. However, an SEC study of selling practices observed that "These [salespeople] are already engaged in unsupervised sales to the public, and the publications, meetings, and seminars, which serve primarily to stimulate sales (and also to remind salesmen of their legal and ethical obligations) may be viewed as methods of sales promotion as well as training."[4]

The SEC also noted:

Because chances are high that his commissions will not reach $1,000 a year, the sales recruit usually continues to have other employment and he will be a part-time salesman. He is encouraged to look to members of his family, relatives, and friends for his first sales. Having exhausted this source, many green salesmen grow discouraged by the process of prospecting, and drift away from the industry. Those with greater persistence may commence to earn higher compensation, become full-time salesmen, and graduate to the ranks of supervisors.[5]

This survey uncovered huge turnover figures among salespeople: Hamilton Management Corporation, with a total of 7,874 salespeople on April 1, 1962, had 2,908 join the firm in 1961 and 2,081 leave; Investors Diversified Services, with 2,863 on April 1, 1962, had 1,107 join as 1,063 left; Mutual Funds Associates, Philadelphia, with 149 salesmen, recruited 70 and lost 53 in one year; and Federated Investors, Pittsburgh, with a total of 449 salespeople at one point, added 219 and lost 322.

Significantly, the study also found a "predominance among those hired of recruits inexperienced in the securities business." At Financial Programs, Denver, Colorado, 302 of the 335 who joined the organization had no prior securities experience. At Triangle Investors Corporation, New York City, 38 of its 52 salespeople were inexperienced newcomers. The Renyx, Field Company, reported that all 123 of its new salespeople were inexperienced and said that experience was "not advantageous to mutual fund sales."

However, general sales experience is considered an asset in a recruit. A manual on the selection, screening, training, and supervision of salespeople states: "The [salesperson] who has had experience in any field requiring systematic prospecting, door-to-door selling, daily recordkeeping, and customer follow-through is by all odds the best recruit, whatever he may have sold in the past." According to this manual, good prospective salespeople can be found among cosmetic, brush, roof-and-siding, real estate, storm window, and food-freezer salespeople, or "any in the gamut of household salespeople."[6]

New salespeople are urged to buy fund shares themselves and to tell prospective buyers they plan to accumulate more as soon as they can. They are told to spread their message to relatives, friends, neighbors, and business acquaintances. As one sales manual put it, "Suppose at the beach you see two men drowning. One is a close friend. Do you help the stranger first or your friend?" Another training course lists 100 questions for salesmen to ask themselves in order to build a list of people to call on. Included in this list are the following:

> Whom do you know from your old job?
> Whom do you know from your church?
> Whom do you know through your children?
> Who sells you your groceries?
> Who is your dentist?
> Who is your best luncheon club friend?
> Who heads the local parent-teacher association?
> Who is your florist?
> Who is your postmaster or letter carrier?
> Who soles your shoes?
> Who heads your bank?
> Who lives next door to you?[7]

According to his instructions, once a sale is made, the sales-person is expected to ask his customer for the names of a few other persons who might benefit from regular fund investments. An alert salesperson, moreover, will find ways of keeping in touch with you. You may count on greeting cards at Christmas and other holidays, congratulatory cards on your birthday and wedding anniversary, and frequent phone calls when the fund has announced an extra dividend or an unusually large increase in assets. You may have made a friend for life.

Several years ago, when selling mutual funds attracted more people than it does today, "cold-turkey" visits to prospective buyers were more common. For the most part, the names were taken from a general list, such as a telephone directory. This approach is known as prospecting.

Advertisements in financial publications are an important source of leads for fund salespeople. And the fund offers a prospectus and annual report to anyone who fills out and returns the coupon in the ad. Usually space is provided for your phone number, but it does not matter whether you fill in this or not. A salesperson will track down your number from the phone directory and insist upon delivering the material personally.

One potential buyer staying temporarily with friends completed a coupon in an advertisement run by Investors Diversified Services, one of the largest fund complexes. The coupon was turned over to a salesperson. Although no phone number was given, the salesperson consulted a special directory profitably sold by the telephone company. Finding a number listed in the friend's name at the address given, he phoned the prospect and requested an appointment. When the prospect said he wanted to read the prospectus and annual report before discuss-ing the matter, the salesperson retorted, "We're not allowed to send out this material. It costs $5 or $6, and we can't give it to everybody." The prospect refused to make an appointment and did not receive the material that the advertisement promised.

Before fund shares are bought, the potential buyer is supposed to receive a prospectus — a detailed description, legally required to be truthful and accurate, of the fund's purposes, methods of operating, advisory and administrative fees, and principal officers. The prospectus may contain damaging information (for example, about its organizers' lack of experience or excessive fees paid to its advisers), which the salesperson would prefer you did not see. Frequently salespeople delivering the prospectus will advise prospective customers that it is complicated and need not be read. Usually it is not. "When you run into a nit-picker, somebody who wants to read every line and question every point before he buys, you know you're going to have trouble," a salesperson confided to me. In truth, fund salespeople do not want informed buyers, for such buyers are apt to question the wisdom of paying high sales and advisory fees for a fund that achieves no more for them than a fund with no sales commission or low advisory fees. As soon as you begin thinking for yourself, the salesperson feels the sale slipping away. The salesperson prefers to give you as little chance for independent thinking as possible.

The salesperson employing good prospecting techniques will try to avoid an initial disclosure that he or she is selling fund shares, an SEC study observed. In telephoning prospects for appointments, salespeople refer to themselves as *financial planners*. If a prospect is cagey and wants to know what the caller is selling, one sales manual instructs the salesperson to reply: "My organization specializes in financial planning. We've helped many families to understand Social Security, its benefits and requirements. We are happy to provide this important service without cost or obligation."

Should the prospect, still suspicious, want to know what the caller will get from all this, the suggested reply is: "Mr. _____, we are compensated only in the event that we assist you with your personal financial planning. However, we are happy to provide important information regarding Social Security, its benefits and requirements without any cost or obligation on your part. Would Tuesday at 8:15 be a good time for me to bring you the form I mentioned, or would Thursday at 8:45 be more convenient?"

A door-opening approach proposed by the *Ideas for New Salesmen* service of Kalb, Voorhis, and Company suggests that salespeople call up old friends or relatives for advice and ask to visit them. Once there the salesperson says he or she has a presentation to try out and would appreciate it if the friend would pretend to be a prospect, ask questions, and listen on that basis.

The *Ideas* service continues:

>The entire presentation should be made with the friends' needs in mind, slanted to college education, retirement, whatever fits best.
>
>The salesman then makes the complete presentation and at the end, may switch with something like — "The more I think of it, George, the more I think *you* really ought to invest in Mutual Funds. I know you'll retire in about _____ years, and it's time you started to do something about it."
>
>The salesman can then switch to the personal completely and go for the close.
>
>If he makes the sale, fine. If not, he will at least get some advice on his presentation, as well as some practice in giving it, and he stands a good chance of getting referrals.[8]

When SEC investigators questioned the propriety of this idea, Ferdinand Nauheim, a partner in the firm that originated it, circumvented the issue and instead eulogized the industry for the important service it performs and the high standards it maintains. Thus Nauheim argued:

>As far as the high standards of what a salesman is taught to do in selling mutual funds, the crucial area is the presentation itself. How he gets someone to listen to him is a different subject because a salesman who becomes imbued with the need for most people to do something to plan for their financial future recognizes the fact that he has to find ways and means to get people to listen to that story. So I think it is well in keeping with the high standards of this business, if a man is sincere about wanting to reach people, with a story that needs to be told, if he does things that may sound to you as though they are tricky, but we who are daily engaged in this business of trying to help people recognize a need, if we are going to get people to hear something that can do them good.[9]

The Rules of the Game

In their sales and promotional literature funds are expressly forbidden to promise shareholders that they can achieve a projected performance. According to an SEC statement of policy set down in November, 1957, it is misleading for investment literature to include the following:

> To represent or imply an assurance that an investor's capital will increase or that purchase of investment company shares involves a preservation of original capital and a protection against loss in value.
>
> To discuss accumulation of capital, preservation of capital, accumulation of an estate, protection against loss of purchasing power, diversification of investments, financial independence or profit possibilities without pointing out or explaining the market risks inherently involved in the investment.
>
> To represent or imply an assurance that an investor will receive a stable, continuous, dependable, or liberal return or that he will receive any specified rate or rates of return.
>
> To make any reference to registration or regulation of any investment company under Federal or state authority without explaining that this does not include supervision of management or investment practices or policies. . . .
>
> To represent or imply that shares of an investment company are similar to or as safe as government bonds, insurance annuities, savings accounts or life insurance, or have the fixed income, principal, or any other features of a debt security.
>
> To represent or imply that the management of an investment company is under the same type of investment restrictions or is operated under limitations similar to or has fiduciary obligations such as those imposed by government authorities on savings banks and insurance companies. . . .
>
> To make any extravagant claims regarding management ability or competency.
>
> To represent or imply that investment companies are operated as, or are similar to, "cooperatives."
>
> To fail to include in any sales literature which does not state the amount or rate of the sales commission . . . a clear reference to the prospectus or prospectuses for information concerning the sales commission, and other information.

The printed promotion material of funds generally abides by these and other SEC restrictions. But because sales literature does not contain the claim that "Mutual funds are the perfect hedge against inflation" does not mean that such claims are not made. The fact is that fund salespeople routinely represent fund shares as the "best way" to accumulate and preserve capital and assure an income in one's old age.

Anyone who has heard a fund salesperson's spiel knows that the funds are not represented according to the objective standards specified by the SEC. The fund salesperson is no different from other salespersons. He plays up the good points of his product and lets you discover the risks for yourself. Citing the fund's glowing record, the salesperson all but guarantees that this record will continue in the future or neglects to warn what will happen to your retirement plans if the market goes into a sharp and prolonged decline around the time you must start drawing on your investment. Fund salespeople would drop out of business by the thousands if they could not bring out their charts to show how their fund did in the past and, by implication, what it will do in the future.

A gambit of salespeople — theoretically forbidden but widely practiced — is to combine a fund's income and capital gains distributions and to call the total the "yield" for the year. Suppose a fund distributed $.40 out of its 1971 dividend income and also distributed $.50 in capital gains. By putting the distributions together, the salesperson implies that the investor got a 9 percent return, more than top-quality bonds yield. The salesperson may not reveal that the distribution represents only one year's results (and, unlike bonds, carried no assurance of being continued in the future). The salesperson may also fail to note that the capital gains distribution may represent profits gained over a period longer than one year.

"Selling dividends" is another fairly common (but forbidden) practice. In this case the salesperson urges a customer to buy shares now because the fund will soon declare a dividend. Of course, the fact that the amount of the dividend is already included in the price at which the shares sell is never revealed. Nor does the salesperson mention that when the dividend becomes payable, the value of each share will drop by the exact amount of the dividend. Instead of gaining by buying before a dividend is declared, the customer actually loses: pays the full price for the dividend and, when it is declared, must pay income tax upon it. Thus the customer gets less than if he or she had bought after the dividend record date. To compound the unfairness of "selling dividends," even the sales commission per share is higher than if the customer had bought after the dividend date.

Theoretically, the salesperson is bound to make certain that you pay the lowest possible commission when you buy fund shares.

The following are percentage sales charges of a typical fund:

Size of purchase	Sales charges (as % of total purchase price)
Less than $25,000	8.5
$25,000 to $49,999	7.5
$50,000 to $99,999	6.0
$100,000 to $249,999	4.5
$250,000 to $499,999	3.0
$500,000 and over	1.5

Some funds have first breakpoints of $15,000; some drop the sales charge to 4 percent at $50,000. Whatever the rates, however, simple arithmetic demonstrates that it is sometimes in the salesperson's best interest, though not the customer's, actually to sell fewer shares. For example, a salesperson selling shares in a fund employing the above rate schedule will profit more from a sale of 24,000 shares than from a sale of 25,000 shares — 8.5 percent of 24,000 is greater than 7.5 percent of 25,000. Nevertheless, the salesperson is supposed to point out that you would do better to buy (or to contract to buy) $25,000 worth of shares even though the salesperson's commission would be less. Hence the temptation not to advise you about this is great.

In a notorious case for which the broker-dealer firm of Mason, Moran and Company had its registration revoked, three of the company's employees had sold more than $500,000 worth of fund shares to an order of nuns at slightly below breakpoints. The funds provided that a lower commission be paid when the purchase was in excess of $25,000. Within one year the broker executed 26 purchase orders, 10 of which were executed on sales of from $23,400 to $24,900. The nuns were never advised of the advantages of buying at the $25,000 point. A trial examiner found that the firm had built up a relationship of "trust and confidence" and used it "to deprive the customer of established and clearly available price benefits in order to swell its own profits."[10]

In compliance with the principle that the securities business should be self-regulating, most of the burden of policing mutual funds sales practices falls on the Investment Companies Committee of the National Association of Security Dealers. However, it is commonly believed that for every 50 salespeople who violate the rules in one way or another, only one gets caught at it. Even when improper selling practices are detected, the penalty imposed on the culprit is rarely severe enough to discourage future improprieties.

In one case a firm committed 187 violations of the statement of policy covering a 4-year period, failed to supervise salespeople, and committed many other violations. The firm was censured and fined $500. Another firm was fined $200 after a finding that its sales literature was misleading and contained 111 statement-of-policy violations. In another case a firm was found to have violated the statement of policy, to have failed to file sales literature, to have practiced the "selling" of dividends, and to have failed to supervise its employees. It was fined $100. In contrast (and indicative of what *really* matters to the NASD), a broker who made one sale of investment company shares below the public offering price was fined $400.[11]

A survey of fund investors conducted by the Securities Research Unit of the Wharton School of Finance and Commerce observed:

> Since mutual fund salesmen generally sell away from their own offices and in the offices and homes of their customers, and since they are generally selling to new customers rather than engaging in continuing transactions for an existing clientele, selling activities of most salesmen appear to be largely unsupervised. The selling organizations have hierarchies of supervisory personnel, but their primary activity is selling, stimulating sales and recruit-

ing, and the control they exercise over the sales tactics of their salesmen is limited. Home office administrative controls, exercised through a review of sales applications at a distance from the point of sale without substantial information concerning the customer's financial status, can at best apply only to the most obvious types of abuse. Only a few companies have established staffs of roving field investigators to check on salesmen, and these staffs are small in size.

Federal controls over mutual fund sales practices include the general antifraud provisions of the securities laws, the disclosure requirements of the securities laws, and the commission's statement of policy covering mutual fund sales literature. While its powers are sufficient to require appropriate sales restraint in the use of the written word, the commission is presented with difficult enforcement problems in the characteristic home selling of mutual funds through oral presentations. In addition, the commission's regular inspection programs are difficult to gear to detection of the type of abuse which may most characteristically occur in the sale of mutual funds.

The NASD is the industry's only self-regulatory body that significantly controls the mutual fund retail sales organizations, although a few of the largest of those organizations that are wholly integrated are not members of that association. The commission looks largely to the NASD for enforcement of the statement of policy, and the NASD has brought a number of disciplinary actions relating to its violation, as well as for charges of switching funds and selling dividends. For the NASD too, however, the home sale of funds makes detection of high-pressure sales a difficult problem.[12]

Are Fund Salespeople Worth Their Cost?

In the final analysis, the basic question is whether fund salespeople justify their commissions. Those who respond in the affirmative base such justification on the grounds that they fit the fund to the customer. With so many different funds available, they argue, it is important to choose the one that meets the buyer's specific investment needs. Thus, a fund that strives for maximum performance with hot stocks that might bomb in a bear market is hardly suitable for the 75-year-old widow who needs safety of capital above all. And the ideal choice for the young investor looking ahead to decades of inflation is not a fund heavily invested in bonds with little or no prospects for growth. The fund salesperson, it is asserted, will find the proper growth fund for the risk-minded youngster as well as the proper income fund for the elderly pensioner.

The Rules of Fair Practice of the NASD stipulate that the recommendation to purchase any security to a customer must be based on reasonable knowledge that the security is suitable for the customer. According to the NASD, the seller cannot be relieved of his responsibility because the customer fails to tell all the facts. Yet investigators of the Wharton School disclosed the disgraceful fact that in 60 percent of cases studied, the sales representative asked *no* questions about the customer's financial circumstances or investment objectives. The researchers surmised: "In many cases prior information which the salesman may have gained through continuing customer-client relationships or close personal ties may satisfy his obligation." But, they concluded, "The proportion of transactions in which the salesman seemingly made no inquiry into investors' financial positions would appear inevitably to involve some violations of the rule."[13]

For the most part, buyers of mutual funds have at best a hazy idea of their commitment. This conclusion was reached by the Wharton survey of investors who had purchased or redeemed fund shares in mid-March and mid-June, 1962. The investors represented a cross-section of buyers of all kinds of mutual funds.

After questioning the investors about the fund's purposes and performance, sales charges paid, the amount the investment charged to manage the fund, and the source of the fund's earnings, the investigators concluded that fund buyers have "only a modest understanding" of their investment:

> The average time devoted to reading the prospectus was a little over an hour for regular purchasers, and a little less than 1½ hours for those who bought contractual plans. Few purchasers apparently made use of information other than that provided by sales representatives of the funds. About 40 percent mentioned other sources of information, but these were mainly friends, relatives, and other purchasers. About 10 percent of purchasers mentioned financial sections of newspapers or other financial publications.

While more purchasers were informed on sales charges than on other elements of their investment security, for most their knowledge was incomplete and often inadequate. Among those who bought funds with sales charges on regular account, about one-eighth apparently thought they paid no sales charge, and an equal proportion did not know whether they did or not. In addition to those who believed that they did not pay a sales charge or did not know whether they did or not, over one-quarter could make no estimate of its amount. Overall, less than 40 percent provided a reasonable estimate of the sales charge they had paid. On the other hand, over 90 percent of those who purchased no-load funds stated that they had paid no such charge.

To determine their understanding of the level and structure of contractual sales charges, planholders were asked to estimate these charges for the first year, during the first 2 years, and over the life of the contract. Forty percent of contractual plan purchasers could make no estimate of the first-year sales charge, and only about two-fifths of purchasers of these plans placed the first-year charge within a reasonable range.[14]

Considerably fewer contractual plan buyers knew the level of the sales charge over the life of the contract; about two-thirds could make no estimate of what it might be. Somewhat fewer than one-fourth of contractual purchasers provided a reasonable estimate. In general, mutual fund buyers had little knowledge of alternatives. Approximately three-quarters of regular purchasers who paid normal sales charges did not know whether there were funds with sales charges that were higher or lower; about the same proportion was unaware of the existence of no-load funds. Among investors in contractual plans, a somewhat higher percentage was unaware that fund shares could be purchased with sales charges different from those of the fund they bought. A similar proportion was unaware of the availability of no-load funds.

Investors' knowledge of their funds' sources of earnings, which the Wharton researchers considered an approximate indication of their understanding of the performance and risk implications of mutual fund investment, was somewhat greater. But a considerable number had clearly misconceived the functions performed by their funds. Almost 20 percent did not know that the funds sought to make earnings or profits from buying and selling securities. About 25 percent thought that sales charges paid by new investors contributed to earnings of their funds. Thirty percent were uncertain on this point. The total of ignorant fund purchasers was thus 75 percent.[15]

The Wharton researchers concluded:

> The evidence suggesting limited ability of most such investors (those who buy load funds) to deal with relevant investment issues is quite clear. A substantial number, in one form or another, were dependent on others in the conduct of their financial affairs. For many investment was a new experience. Some, perhaps swayed by the glamour and excitement of market participation, failed to undertake a careful financial analysis. A considerable proportion are drawn from unskilled occupations, persons with limited education, low-income groups, the retired or elderly women — many of whom are widows. A high proportion buy their shares from salesmen who are also close friends or relatives. This suggests that the detachment and circumspection required of an alert buyer frequently may be missing. These and other equally marked indications of a lack of expertness in financial matters may suggest that additional safeguards may be required for the protection of investors in mutual funds.[16]

The data that formed the basis of this survey were obtained in 1962. Nothing in the record, and certainly nothing in experience and observation, would lead to the conclusion that the person to whom fund shares are sold — as opposed to the person who seeks out shares on his own — has changed at all.

Taking the Teeth Out of Front-End Loads

Until a few years ago the main gun in the sales arsenal was the contractual plan. Under this plan the customer, in exchange for agreeing to buy fund shares over an extended period of time, was given a lower commission rate. But commissions for the agreed-upon purchases — the "front-end" load — were deducted from the first payments so that little of the customer's money went into actual investments. A customer who dropped out of the plan lost the commission money already paid on share purchases not yet made.

The disadvantages such plans present for customers were summarized by the SEC:

These plans are basically long-range programs for investing in the shares of a particular mutual fund on an installment basis but with the unique feature that the purchaser is required to pay a substantial portion of the total sales charge in advance (the front-end load). As a consequence of this front-end load a purchaser in essence commits himself to purchase shares of a particular mutual fund over a period of time — typically 10 years — on the basis of information concerning the fund supplied to him at the time he makes his first purchase. If adverse personal circumstances render the purchaser financially unable to continue his purchases, if his investment objective changes, if the fund no longer enjoys his confidence, or if for any other reason he no longer wishes to invest in the fund, he discontinues his purchases only at the cost of a penalty. In this respect contractual plans, which contemplate a commitment to purchase securities far in the future on the basis of information received in the present, are an exception to and appear somewhat inconsistent with the underlying philosophy of the securities laws that an investor shall have current information available to him at the time of purchasing securities on which to base his investment decision.

The security which the contractual plan purchaser acquires is much more complex than that acquired by the direct purchase of mutual fund shares. The prospectus which describes what the contractual plan purchaser has bought (and what it costs him) is typically longer and more difficult to understand than the prospectus which is delivered to the direct purchaser of mutual fund shares. Paradoxically, a substantial number of these complex securities are sold to the least sophisticated portion of the investing public. A high proportion of contractual plan purchasers are making their first purchase of equity securities. Many of them are persons in low-income brackets with heavy family responsibilities and no financial resources apart from their wages or salaries. A large proportion of these persons do not understand the amount or the impact of the front-end load. They are, for the most part, unaware that mutual fund shares may be acquired in a less expensive way through a voluntary or level-load plan or through no-load plans.

The sale of complex securities to unsophisticated investors in a way which permits the investor fully to understand and evaluate the intricate merchandise he is acquiring is at best a difficult task. High-pressure selling, inadequate training of and lack of adequate supervision and control over salesmen, all of which appear to be present to a high degree in the sale of contractual plans, make its accomplishment most unlikely. The front-end load structure encourages high-pressure selling. The substantial commission which a salesman receives from the initial 13 payments, particularly when the purchaser prepays a number of them as he is usually urged to do, gives the salesman a strong incentive to sell these plans regardless of the circumstances of the purchaser in order to realize commissions on at least the front-end portion of the load.[17]

Many well-documented studies reveal how many investors have suffered serious losses through such plans. In 1962 researchers examined the results of contractual plans begun in February, 1959, three and one-half years before. Of all contractual plan purchasers, one-sixth of those who had failed to keep up the required payments or had redeemed their shares paid one dollar in sales commissions for every dollar actually invested in fund shares. Another sixth of all plan purchasers redeemed their shares or lapsed in their payments. Ultimately, they paid an effective sales load of more than 18 percent.

The results of another study made in the 1960s indicated that 15 percent of contractual plan purchasers redeemed their shares within 5 years of their original purchases. And all took a loss, despite the fact that stock prices generally rose during that period.[18]

In 1970 Congress provided that dissatisfied purchasers of contractual plans with front-end loads could demand a full refund of the extra sales charges within forty-five days of signing for the plan and a partial refund if they decide to terminate it within 18 months.

According to a supplementary SEC ruling, whenever investors in such plans miss 3 payments before the contract is 15 months old, sponsors of the plans must send them a notice informing them of the refund to which they are entitled if they drop out. As a result, contractual plans have become much less profitable for fund salespeople — and selling funds has become a less appealing occupation.

Members of Congress have received hundreds of complaints from mutual fund buyers about sales charges, about losses sustained when fund shares had to be sold before their value appreciated enough to cover the sales load, and about the failure of funds to perform as salespeople promised. Some of these letters were put into the record of House committee hearings on mutual funds by Representative John E. Moss of California, chairman of the subcommittee on Commerce and Finance. Among them were the following three complaints:

> I am buying shares in Manhattan Fund, with a plan to use them for retirement about 10 years away. Each month, some salesman gets 8 percent of my savings even though he no longer does anything to serve me. I send my checks to the bank, and they send me a receipt after sending him 8 percent for nothing!

> Just a few months ago I invested in four funds after considerable research. All the brokerage did was sign the application blank and continue to collect fees.

> Our one dissatisfaction is with the sales charge. We never saw our salesman again after the first evening — there was no need as the investments are made by mail. He has never rendered any services of any kind. Our only contact is a Christmas card from him once a year. Our cash investments have totaled $6,700, and our dividends, $463 plus. At the present 8½% sales charge, we have paid $608 for one evening's counseling — and shall continue to pay with all subsequent investments. This is an absurdity and out of all proportion.[19]

Some fund defenders claim that they "save their customers from themselves." In 1967, Cornelius Roach, chairman of the Board of the Association of Mutual Fund Plan Sponsors, testified before a congressional committee that the "primary objective" of contractual plans consisted of "putting aside savings amounting to billions of dollars which those investors would otherwise have spent as disposable income."[20]

The "Insurance Against Loss" Gimmick

Another gimmick to improve fund sales consists of insurance against a decline in the value of fund shares. In May, 1971, the National Securities and Research Corporation announced that it had reached an agreement with the Harleysville Mutual Insurance Company, Harleysville, Pennsylvania, to insure shareholders against loss in the Fairfield Fund, which it manages. Not long afterward several dozen other funds announced that they would offer similar coverage.

In theory, the Fairfield plan is appealing: you pay a total insurance premium of 6 percent on your investment plus an annual administrative charge of .2 percent of the funds you buy up to a maximum of $12 a year. Should you want to insure a $3,000 investment for 10 years, your total cost would be $240 — $180 for the insurance and $60 for administration costs. This amounts to $24 annually, or .008 of your original investment per year. Sponsors of the program claim the insurance payments are painless because they are taken out of dividends and capital gains distributed by the funds.

However, critics have found several things wrong with the plan. First, the insurance charges are based on the assumption that you will hold the fund shares for the full period of coverage, which may be 10, 12.5, or 15 years. If you must sell your shares before that time at a loss, your coverage is not effective and all insurance payments also are lost. Practically, then, you had better not need the money until the insurance period expires.

Perhaps the greatest objection is that your insurance is only as sound as your insurance company. A catastrophic stock market, producing gigantic losses like those of 1929, might produce such a strain that the insurance company could not make the promised loss payments. This possibility probably would not daunt the more enterprising fund salespeople, however. No doubt they would then sell insurance to protect your insurance.

Fund Shares for Your Heirs?

Although defenders of the fund industry usually stress the value of fund shares in a retirement program, they fail to mention that shares in a load fund may be most undesirable in an estate. This condition arises as a result of a quirk in the United States Treasury laws.

Under a regulation promulgated in 1963, the Internal Revenue Service decreed that in order to compute estate and gift taxes, mutual fund shares must be valued at their *replace-*

ment cost. The replacement cost is defined as the amount a new buyer would pay, and it consists of the *offering price,* the net asset value of the shares plus the sales commission. The heirs must pay a tax on the higher figure, although they will receive only the lower "bid price" when they redeem their shares. This seeming injustice is eased somewhat by reductions in the offering price to correspond with lower commissions payable when large amounts of funds shares are bought. Thus the spread between bid and asked prices on $50,000 worth of funds might be only 4 instead of 8½ percent.

The IRS method of valuing fund shares may produce a minor windfall for the heirs if the total estate is below the level at which federal estate taxes are levied ($60,000 or $120,000, depending upon marital status). For example, consider an estate valued at $50,000 that includes mutual funds worth $20,000 if redeemed. In this case the replacement cost of the funds would be $21,700. Although no federal tax is payable on the shares, they are appraised at the higher value. Assume that the heir sells his shares at $25,000. Since his replacement cost was $21,700, his official gain — and therefore his tax — would be less than if the shares were valued only at $20,000.

On the other hand, mutual fund shares offer a fairly easy means of minimizing probate costs. These are the legal costs involved in processing a will. Such a procedure is necessary in order to assure that assets are distributed to the intended parties. Probate costs can be heavy. Theoretically they are determined by the amount of work a lawyer must do to clear up an estate. Often, they are more directly related to the value of the estate involved in probate. One legal reference service has estimated that such costs, including probate court costs and all fees of lawyers, executors, and appraisers, may run to 10 percent of an estate below $100,000. That amounts to a fat $5,000 on a $50,000 estate. Its estimate of average probate costs on a $100,000 estate runs to about 8.2 percent; of an estate of $500,000, about 7 percent; of a $1 million estate, 6.4 percent; and of a $2 million estate, 6 percent. This amount does not include estate taxes.

Given the relationship between probate costs and the value

of assets covered by the will, the way to reduce such costs is to arrange to have your assets transferred to your heirs without going through the probate courts. One way is to put your securities in a "living trust" in their name. You retain use of the money while you live, but at your death the shares automatically revert to them. As they do not pass through your will, they also bypass probate costs. For estate tax purposes these trusts are added to your other assets upon your death. Hence some of the money you keep from the legal profession may be taken by the tax collector. On balance, however, the more you keep from probate, the more your heirs receive. Many funds provide forms to enable purchasers to buy their shares in trust.

6

Games the Fund Managers Play — with Your Money

You are the portfolio manager for the XYZ Growth Fund. You have examined the record and prospects of the Misanthropic Computer Company and have decided that its new methods of dunning customers for the money that they owe their utility for gas and electricity will revolutionize the industry. You want to buy 100,000 shares, but the company has only 2.5 million shares outstanding — more than half of them in the hands of the firm's founders — and you know that once you start buying for your fund, its present $10 price per share will rise sharply. Yet the company's prospects are so good that you will go as high as $15 for its shares.

The thought hits you that *someone* who knew your intentions might make an easy 50 percent profit by buying MCC before the fund placed its order. The person might even double his or her money by buying the shares on 50 percent margin. If you play the game ethically, of course, the thought will leave your mind as quickly as it entered. "Taking advantage of inside

information in advance of fund transactions for personal gains"
is not done, in theory. You are supposed to have your shareholders' interests at heart, and buying shares ahead of the fund
tends to raise the price that they (indirectly) will pay for them.
Nevertheless, you face payments on your new Mercedes and
your summer place at East Hampton; and a quick $20,000
profit could help allay any twinges of conscience caused by doing
the unethical. Besides, your brother-in-law's wife's cousin is
a discreet sort who likes to play the market. In return for a
little participation for himself, he could be persuaded to buy
3,000 shares for you through his broker in Seattle, 4,000 miles
away. No one else would know what you had done. Do you
declare yourself the winner in this not uncommon conflict
of interest?

It seems fair to say that most investment company insiders —
officers, directors, and employees with advance information of
plans to buy or sell — resist the temptation to make extra
money for themselves. Moreover, funds frequently lack the
power exhibited by the XYZ Fund to move prices dramatically.
When, as often happens, funds buy and sell large blocks of
stock with each other, the market price usually does not budge.
If tens of millions of shares of a company's stock are in public
hands, a fund may buy 200,000 shares in small lots in the open
market and still pay less for its last shares than its first ones.
Nevertheless, opportunities exist (or seem to exist) for insiders
to profit by purchasing stocks before their fund begins dealing
in them. Despite official and unofficial statements that this kind
of trading is "inconsistent with the obligations of fund executives and employees to their investment company," there is
evidence to prove its existence. Moreover, many Wall Streeters
suspect that such trading (through devices such as using one's
brother-in-law's wife's cousin to handle the transaction) is
more widespread than the evidence would indicate.

The available records indicate that many fund insiders
confirm Oscar Wilde's observation that the best way to get rid
of temptation is to give in to it. In one study the SEC found that
as many as 14.4 percent of the persons and companies surveyed
had bought or sold securities that were at the same time being
actively traded in by the fund with which they were associated.

Eight percent had traded within fifteen days prior to the fund's trading. Trading following transactions of the investment company was reported by 20.7 percent of all persons and companies surveyed.[1]

"It is clear that fairly extensive trading [by insiders] in mutual fund portfolio securities does take place," the official report of the study concluded. The report stated:

> The survey of a large number of persons and firms having access to fund investment recommendations and decisions for a substantial and representative group of mutual funds showed trading in portfolio securities over a brief 7-month period by at least 30 percent of the respondents. In an individual firm as many as 11 different people traded in at least 28 different securities during that period. Much of the insider trading revealed by the survey, of course, may have been consistent with the best interests of the funds themselves. However, the substantial number of insiders executing transactions before or during the funds' trading date range gives evidence of the existence of some trading which, consciously or unconsciously, was inconsistent with the best interests of the funds.
>
> To a major extent, the insider trading disclosed by the survey involved modest numbers of shares and dollars. Even where the price differentials were small and the number of shares involved almost nominal, trades might involve a situation of conflicting interests. On the other hand, the difficulties of drawing lines and measuring injury suggest that even minor instances of advantaging the insider should not be condoned by the industry. If the mutual fund industry, like Caesar's wife, is to be above suspicion, it cannot fail to be concerned with the extent of insider trading shown, regardless of the petty amounts involved in some of it, and with the extent to which industry's announced policies appear to be ignored.[2]

Norman F. Dacey, who has been identified with mutual funds for a third of a century as an organizer, administrator, and salesperson, charged before a Congressional committee that "too many" fund managers profited privately from their positions. He said:

> Too many portfolio managers are receiving private deals and kickbacks, particularly in the area of negotiated transactions involving letter stock. Too many portfolio managers are buying

stock privately today which they intend to begin buying for their fund tomorrow. They know that in the course of building the fund's position in the stock, they will run its price up to their own advantage. As it is presently written, the law does not tell them that they cannot do these things. It assumes that they will recognize them as dishonest practices. Obviously, that assumption is not valid.[3]

Excessive Commissions

A fund may pay excessive commissions when its fund manager engages in "interpositioning." A 1967 case involving the Delaware Management Company provides an example. This company is the principal investment adviser and underwriter for the Decatur Fund and the Delaware Income Funds. The SEC has charged that between October, 1961, and September, 1966, the management company placed 400 trading orders with Mutual Funds Associates, a broker-dealer, Mutual sold large numbers of Delaware and Decatur shares but did not make markets in the portfolio securities. It forwarded the trade orders to other brokers, pocketing a commission for its efforts.

In almost every instance the funds were in a position to deal directly with the same broker-dealers who ultimately executed the trades. Had they done so, the funds would not have incurred the costs charged to them by Mutual. Indeed, the funds occasionally traded with these broker-dealers.

The SEC said also that members of the advisory firm caused the Delaware Fund to sell 202,000 shares of stock of Libby, McNeill and Libby at $13.50 per share on one day in 1965 through a broker-dealer firm, although another broker-dealer had simultaneously offered $14. The executing broker was chosen because it had provided the adviser with research and statistical services, while the other firm neither supplied such services nor sold the fund's shares. The sale of the Libby stock at the lower price, it was charged, was designed to benefit the adviser at the expense of the fund and its shareholders.

The SEC charged that the "interpositioning" and the Libby transactions constituted fraud. The Delaware Management Company agreed to pay $319,127 to the funds to reimburse them for their excess costs. Though the company did not admit or deny the alleged violations, it accepted a 45-day suspension, and its officers accepted suspensions of up to 60 days.[4]

Commenting on the case, an SEC report said:

> The execution of portfolio transactions of investment companies through some broker-dealers who sell their shares has become a well-established practice. Implicit in any consideration of the propriety of a reciprocal practice of this nature is the overriding requirement that the investment company and its shareholders benefit and certainly that they not be injured. Where transactions are effected in a manner calculated to promote the sale of investment company shares, at the cost of sacrificing the best executions on portfolio transactions, the ultimate effect is to increase the cost of securities purchased and reduce the amount for securities sold as compared with the costs and proceeds they might reasonably have expected to realize. While there may be certain economies of size, it should be emphasized that such growth cannot be promoted at the expense of shareholders.[5]

Trading on Secret Information

Mutual funds and other large investors are not legally entitled to access to any information about a company that is not equally available to everyone. There is no such thing as legitimate "inside information." The SEC has served notice that it intends to penalize fund managers to the full if it finds that they have bought or sold on the basis of facts not revealed to the general public.

A significant test case that clearly prescribed the use of "inside information" concluded in July, 1971, with the SEC commissioners' upholding the censure of 12 investment advisers for funds and other groups. They were found to have taken advantage of a broker's tip-off that Douglas Aircraft Corporation would soon release a disappointing earnings report.

A federal examiner reconstructed the case. He reported that early in 1966 many analysts had advised the public to buy Douglas stock since they expected a big earnings gain. The company, a leading producer of commercial aircraft, had estimated its prospective per share earnings at $4 to $4.50 for 1966 and $8 to $12 for 1967. It planned a public offering of Douglas debentures and the brokerage firm of Merrill Lynch,

Pierce, Fenner and Smith was expected to handle the underwriting.

On June 20, 1966, a Douglas official told the Merrill Lynch vice-president in charge of the proposed underwriting that the previously publicized earnings estimates were too optimistic. He said that Douglas had suffered an actual loss in May, that earnings for the first half-year would be only $.49 a share, that it would merely break even in 1966, and that 1967 earnings would be only $5 to $6. The next day this information was relayed to the broker's aerospace analyst; he forwarded it to two salespeople in Merrill Lynch's institutional sales office in New York. They told three other Merrill Lynch employees and, between June 21 and June 23 the five began phoning mutual fund managers who had expressed interest in buying debentures and in some cases had also recently bought Douglas common stock.

Those people favored with this information promptly sold 133,400 shares of Douglas stock from long positions — virtually all they had — and sold short another 21,100 shares. All told, they sold stock worth $13.3 million. The price per share had been as high as 90 on June 21, and despite all the selling pressure, the price rose half a point the next day. (The public was buying heavily, thanks to optimistic newspaper stories about the future of the aerospace industry.) On June 24 Douglas publicly revealed its depressed earnings prospects. The price of Douglas stock dropped to 76 and fell another 7 points the next day. By October it was down to 30.

Among those tippees making a painless exit was the Madison Fund. Relying on the favorable assessments of Douglas's earnings prospects, it had bought 6,000 shares in early June. On June 13 the fund told Merrill Lynch it was considering buying some of the soon-to-be-offered debentures. On June 21, however, it abruptly changed its opinion. Within fifteen minutes after a call from a Merrill Lynch employee, it placed an order to sell all its shares immediately.

Investors Management Company, an investment adviser to several mutual funds, also experienced a sudden change of heart. Between January and April of that year, it had been responsible for a total of 121,000 Douglas shares bought by two funds under its management. After calls by Merrill Lynch salesmen on the afternoon of June 21 and the morning of June 22, IMC advised dumping the entire holding. Some of the holding was sold on June 22, and the remainder was sold within the next three days.

Van Strum and Towne, investment adviser to the Channing Growth Fund, had been responsible for the purchase of 1,500 Douglas shares on June 20. Two days later, at a luncheon for professional investors, the firm's president overheard a comment that Douglas would soon announce zero earnings. Checking out the rumor, he learned that calls were being made by Merrill Lynch. He then called the brokerage house himself, learned what the figures would be, and promptly sold 1,500 shares.

In upholding a censure of the brokerage firm and mutual funds involved, the SEC commented:

We consider that one who obtains possession of material, non-public corporate information, which he has reason to know emanates from a corporate source, and which by itself places him in a position superior to other investors, thereby acquires a relationship with respect to that information within the purview and restraints of the antifraud provisions. Both elements are here present. When a recipient of such corporate information, knowing or having reason to know that the corporate information is non-public, nevertheless uses it to effect a transaction in the corporation's securities for his own benefit, we think his conduct cannot be viewed as free of culpability under any sound interpretation or application of the antifraud provisions. . . .

We do not find persuasive the claim that persons managing funds of others had a fiduciary duty to their clients to sell their Douglas stock upon learning of the poor Douglas earnings, and that a failure to do so might have subjected them to liability for breach of such duty. The obligations of a fiduciary do not include performing an illegal act, and they could have sold the Douglas stock in a legal manner if they had secured the public disclosure of the information by Douglas. And there is no basis for the stated concern that a fiduciary who refrains from acting because he has received what he believes to be restricted information would be held derelict if it should later develop that the information could in fact have been acted upon legally. If that belief is reasonable, his non-action could not be held improper.[6]

The Parvin/Dohrmann Caper

A chilling example of the dangerous games some fund managers play with other people's money was provided in the case of the Parvin/Dohrmann Company. Parvin/Dohrmann is a supplier of kitchen equipment to hotels and restaurants and the owner of two Las Vegas hotels and gambling casinos — the Fremont and the Aladdin.

In August, 1968, Delbert Coleman, the multimillionaire former president of the Seeburg Corporation, began negotiations to acquire a substantial interest in Parvin/Dohrmann. Coleman was apparently attracted to this company by its report for the first half of 1968, which showed that the rate of earnings had doubled over the comparable period of 1967. The company officials had buoyantly predicted that earnings for the full year would triple, or even quadruple, those of 1967. Coleman acquired a controlling block of Parvin/Dohrmann stock at $35 per share.

Stories began circulating in the mutual fund industry that big things were happening at Parvin/Dohrmann. As the SEC reconstructed the story in a 48-page complaint, Coleman advised his broker friends that the firm planned to acquire more Las Vegas hotel casinos and that these acquisitions could boost earnings per share by $9 a year. John Dunphy, a partner of Jesup and Lamont, a New York brokerage firm with many mutual fund clients, repeated the story to a portfolio manager for J. M. Hartwell and Company, a fund adviser to the Hartwell and Campbell funds. Hartwell and Company then bought 16,700 shares for institutional and advisory clients. Meetings with officials of Allen and Company resulted in several big sales. Once Coleman purchased 3,700 shares in a trade recorded on the American Stock Exchange and resold them to Allen in a private transaction. A Parvin/Dohrmann director also sold another 15,000 shares "off the floor." Such activities can falsify the supply-demand picture about a stock: demand shows up in the exchange transactions, strengthening its price, but distribution, which could weaken its price, proceeds silently. The SEC later alleged that the purpose of the move, as well as the effect, was manipulation of the stock's prices.

Coleman and William Scott, Parvin/Dohrmann's president,

met with Dunphy and William Suter, another Jesup and Lamont partner, in Las Vegas in February, 1969. Coleman and Scott told them that while Parvin/Dohrmann might report a loss for 1968 due to the write-down of certain assets, dramatically improved earnings could be expected in 1969. At Hartwell's request, Dunphy and Suter relayed this information to a portfolio manager. Dunphy also predicted big earnings gains in 1970. Hartwell and Company bought more than 12,000 shares between February 18 and March 1. Jesup and Lamont bought 19,000 shares for their clients.

Shortly thereafter, according to the SEC, Tsai Management Company got into the act. Scott told a Tsai analyst that Parvin/Dohrmann would write off $3.5 million in the last quarter but that the first quarter of 1969 would show substantial improvements. Between March 3 and March 17 the Tsai firm bought 49,000 shares for 3 funds under its management: the Manhattan Fund, Fundex, and T.M.R. Appreciation Fund. During the same period Jesup and Lamont purchased over 26,000 shares for institutional clients.

In March, Jesup and Lamont sent a letter to 179 institutional customers, predicting that Parvin/Dohrmann earnings "should show quite a dramatic pattern this year and next." Scott and the controller of Parvin/Dohrmann then met with a Tsai analyst in Los Angeles and gave him detailed financial information including a breakdown of estimated pretax earnings for 1969. Over the next ten days, Tsai Management bought 6,500 additional shares for its funds. After a Tsai analyst shared his new information with a portfolio manager at Hartwell, the latter bought 27,000 more shares within three weeks.

By then Parvin/Dohrmann stock was bubbling, and the daily market stories in the newspapers mentioned it repeatedly. On March 27 the American Stock Exchange halted trading of the stock and urged the corporation to explain the reason for such activity. The company issued a press release stating, among other things, that "the management of the company cannot and has not made any statements to any persons as to the company's financial prospects or financial future."

Later the SEC complaint against Parvin/Dorhmann *et al.* charged that on April 18, 19, and 20 at a Las Vegas meeting

arranged by Coleman, Scott, and Dunphy, 18 representatives
from large institutions and broker-dealers catering to institutions
were guests of Parvin/Dohrmann. Within the next three days
Hartwell bought 34,000 shares for its advisory accounts, Tsai
bought 15,000 for its various funds, and Jesup bought 7,000
for its other clients. With these three buyers accounting for
one-third of all trading, the stock jumped from 109 to 128.

Little of substance seemed to justify such price rises, and the
activity began to alarm officials of the American Stock Exchange.
They feared that this accumulation of shares in the hands of
institutions — accompanied by widespread publicity about
this "hot" stock — could push prices still higher and ultimately
cause huge losses for those who bought shares at that time.

The ASE suspended trading in Parvin/Dohrmann on April
24 and formally asked the SEC to investigate. The latter
suspended trading in the over-the-counter market as well. But
both suspensions were lifted when Coleman issued a statement
"fully disclosing" his company's position.

In October, however, the SEC put together a complaint
charging wholesale illegalities by 13 individuals, 3 corporations,
1 bank, and 1 brokerage firm. Coleman and Scott were accused
of fraudulent manipulation of the price of Parvin/Dohrmann
stock, and Jesup, Lamont, and John Dunphy were accused of
aiding and abetting them. According to the complaint, the four
men "effected transactions intended arbitrarily and artificially to
influence the market price for Parvin/Dohrmann stock and to
maintain, dominate, control, and manipulate the market . . . and
provided [large investors] with material nonpublic information."

Without admitting the allegations Coleman, Scott, and
Parvin/Dohrmann immediately consented to an injunction,
but Dunphy and Jesup and Lamont said that they planned
to fight.

Commenting on the Parvin/Dohrmann case, *Fortune* magazine remarked:

> The SEC's allegations add up to an extraordinary picture of
> the way in which some institutional investors make important
> decisions. The SEC's narrative also sheds light on the clannishness
> among these investors, and shows how easy it is to start a specula-
> tive epidemic in their ranks. Further, it implies a certain lack of

prudent judgment on the part of some professional money managers. Indeed, having read the SEC's lengthy narrative and regarded the position in which some funds now find themselves in relation to Parvin/Dohrmann stock, a man might be tempted to conclude that he could do that well by himself.[7]

Fortune also made the following observations about big institutional buyers' proclivities for instant performance:

> When they believe that they are among the first to learn about a company's ambitious and attractive plans, they may buy in — not so much because they have strong convictions that the plans will work out but because they think others will respond to the spreading news the same way they do. . . . It doesn't seem to matter very much whether what the fund manager hears is accurate or not — as long as he is right in his assumption about the behavior of the competitive institutions. After all, he figures, he can always sell out before the hard and sometimes disappointing facts about corporate earnings are in.[8]

There are numerous other games that fund managers play. The SEC claimed, for example, that from January, 1967, to June, 1968, the Hubsham Management Corporation, a registered broker-dealer acting as investment adviser and principal underwriter for the Hubsham Fund

> . . . allocated portions of brokerage in connection with the fund's portfolio transactions to certain persons, and those persons kicked back some of the proceeds to the management company; caused the fund to pay directly certain expenses of the management company; and in offering and selling the fund's shares put out prospectuses which were false and misleading in failing to disclose these activities, and that the manager had interests adverse to the fund and its shareholders in the allocation and consummation of the fund's portfolio transactions.

Louis Hubsham, Jr., head of both the management company and the fund, consented to the SEC findings without either admitting or denying them. He accepted an order suspending the management company's broker-dealer registration for 30 days and suspending himself from associating with a broker, dealer, or investment adviser for the same period. The management company also agreed to pay the fund $63,351 as com-

pensation for give-ups it had received in connection with the
fund's portfolio transactions; to forego $36,000 in investment
advisory fees; and to pay 20 percent of the rent paid by the
fund in the past which the management company had shared.

In 1969 the SEC commenced administrative proceedings
against the Provident Fund for Income. It alleged that the
fund's registration statement had failed to disclose that Douglas
K. Porteous, president of the fund and of Porteous and
Company, a registered broker-dealer, had arranged a kickback
to Porteous and Company from other broker-dealers; that some
fund brokerage business went to the Pennsylvania Funds Corporation, a registered broker-dealer owned by Porteous himself;
and that Porteous and Company received "tender fees" for
handling some of the fund's portfolio securities in tender
offerings. The fund agreed to the commission's stop order.

In a 1969 action the SEC proceeded against Mates Financial
Services (MFS), a registered investment adviser; Mates Management Company (MMC), the investment adviser of Mates
Investment Fund; and Frederic S. Mates, sole proprietor,
president, and a director of MFS and president of MMC.
According to SEC charges, MFS and Mates gave the securities
business of his advisory clients to brokers who kicked back
substantial rebates purportedly for an investment advisory
publication. He also falsely told his clients that he received no
commissions on their portfolio transactions and that annual
investment advisory fees would not exceed 2 percent of the
net value of securities held.

The commission also alleged that Mates had represented to
shareholders that the fund would not acquire restricted securities (so-called letter stock, which cannot be sold without a
long and costly registration procedure). Nevertheless, he had
the fund acquire substantial amounts of these securities at
lower than the market price although the stock was freely
marketable. Then he marked up the value of the restricted
securities and "misrepresented to shareholders of the fund and
clients and prospective clients of MFS that the resulting net
asset increase was due to his investment advice."

Mates waived a hearing and consented to the SEC allegations.
Accordingly, the commission prohibited Mates from associating

with a broker-dealer without its approval; it suspended the registration of Mates Financial Services as an investment adviser for 100 days; and it prohibited Mates and his financial services from "issuing research reports and performing similar services for broker-dealers for compensation" without prior approval.

The Thundering Herd

One of the most troubling aspects of fund management is the tendency of fund managers to think and act alike. In a speech before a group of investment bankers in 1967, SEC Commissioner Hugh F. Owens observed that the growth of the funds and other institutions has substituted the investment decisions of a few professional managers with control over large blocks of securities for the decisions of large numbers of individual investors. Decisions of individual investors tend to be heterogeneous: they differ widely in their information and ability to analyze the facts at hand as well as in their motivations to buy or sell. Hence their buy and sell orders are usually in rough balance. Any imbalances generally can be handled by the market activity of professionals. Although prices fluctuate, fluctuations from order to order tend to be close to the previous price.

In recent years, with the growth of mutual funds and the increased interest of pension fund and foundation managers in common stocks, the market increasingly has become a trading place for professionals. More than 50 percent of all transactions on the New York Exchange now are executed by "professional money managers" for mutual funds as well as for banks and bank trusts, pension funds, college foundations, and other institutions. Member trading accounts for another 25 percent of the transactions, and individual investors for the balance.

To a great extent, professional managers *make* the market. When they decide as a group that prices are going up and begin to accumulate shares, the absence of sellers produces a sharp upward spiral. Thus the funds can fulfill their own prophecies.

Due to fund managers' similarity in background and approach, says SEC commissioner Owens, their investment decisions "tend to be homogeneous." The following is a common scenario: A fund manager, determined to sell a large block quickly, is unable to find institutional purchasers at or near the last price; he also fails to sell his stock to the public through a secondary distribution. His only recourse is to throw it on the market. But the stock exchange cannot readily absorb all the shares; hence the price drops sharply. As other funds see the stock weakening, they panic and dump their own holdings.

Owens cited the following results of the herd instinct at work:

> On a single day in the fall of 1966, well over 500,000 shares of the stock of one of the so-called glamour stocks were traded on the New York Stock Exchange. Trading in the issue opened at the high for the day and then skidded 16%, closing that day down 19⅝ points. Now what did the funds have to do with that? Mutual funds bought 1,500 shares (about ¼ of 1% of the day's trading) of that company during that day. But mutual funds sold nearly a quarter of a million shares (43.5%) of the day's trading volume on that day. Among these sales by the funds were one block of 25,000 shares sold at 115¼, another block of 32,000 shares sold at 114, and a third block of 137,000 shares sold at 109½.
>
> In the summer of 1966, another of the glamour stocks declined 8%, or 17½ points, in two days. During that two-day decline, mutual funds sold over 130,000 shares of this company, approximately 44.7% of the two-day trading volume in the issue. True, some funds bought the stock as its price was skidding. But those fund purchases amounted in the aggregate to only about 50,000 shares, just about 37% of the massive volume of fund selling.
>
> During seven trading days in the fall of 1966, another common stock declined 32½ points, from 151½ to 119 so that the market value of the stock fell by more than 20% in little more than a week. During this decline, aggregate mutual fund sales of about 70,000 shares accounted for 45.15% of the total trading volume. Mutual funds did some buying during this period. They bought 3,000 shares, just about 4% of the number of shares that they had sold.[9]

Developments in computer technology have intensified the tendency of funds to travel in packs. According to its devotees, computerized research sniffs out market trends with lightning-like rapidity. Digesting such raw figures as the volume of trading and the intensity of up or down movements accompanying such trading, presumably the computer can quickly detect a buying or selling trend that is drying up or a market turn in the making. Some computer buffs take credit for the upturn in prices that most observers attribute to the widely ranging economic reforms announced by President Nixon in August, 1971. They claim that some computer services discerned an imminent price change four days before. According to them, although the Dow-Jones industrials had dropped to 840 (110 points below the high for the year) and many analysts had forecast a continuing decline, some computer services still saw signs of decreased selling pressure and steady accumulation — the earmarks of a rally. They wired their clients (predominantly institutions) to buy for at least a short-term rally. At the time of the president's announcement the averages already were 30 points above their low.

Computerized research tends to encourage speedy investment decisions. Its value depends upon its ability to pick up signals before they become generally visible. To profit from these signals the investor must act quickly. This need for speed, in addition to the increased pressure on fund managers to out-perform their colleagues, is largely responsible for the sharp rises and drops characteristic of the market in recent years. It also accounts for the stomach-churning gyrations in individual stocks.

Reliance upon technical indicators causes market movements to feed upon themselves. Assume that signs are detected of growing selling pressure. Acting on this warning signal, some funds begin to sell. Their selling intensifies the bearish signal, and other funds act upon it. Soon a full-fledged retreat is under way. Many observers have warned that the decision-making procedures of many institutions pose threats of a market panic — the heedless dumping of stock solely because others are dumping. An example of such mindless dumping occurred in April and May, 1970, when heavy selling by funds helped to push the Dow-Jones Average down to 630, or 150 points in two months.

Defenders of investment companies claimed in past years that their professional managers provided a stabilizing force. According to this view, when the uninformed masses of investors feverishly sought to dump their stocks, the cool fund experts would step in to buy the bargains littering the landscape. Similarly, whereas little investors frantically tried to buy stocks and push prices beyond all reasonable limits, the professionals would recognize "overbought" conditions and sell.

However, as massive fund buying and selling has made the market more volatile, the "little investor" has applied the brakes and kept prices from gyrating even more wildly. For years odd-lot investors had regularly sold more stock than they had bought, but they became heavy buyers as the institutions sold in April and May, 1970. In fact, their heavy buying in May, 1970, signaled the market's turnaround.

Some fund managers admit in private that they often cannot resist a stampede. As one fund manager described it:

> You know that the rise or fall in asset value per share is watched every day — and compared with the rise or fall in other funds. Suppose the market starts moving up, but you suspect it won't go up for long. So you keep your cash out of it and watch while the other fellow's assets are rising faster. Maybe you can hold out for a while, but sooner or later the pressure bears down. You begin thinking you'd better go for those big pluses too, or start looking for another job.

The pressure to sell is even greater when everybody else is selling. The fund manager said further:

> Lots of shareholders who buy mutual funds are sold on the idea that the fund manager won't make the mistakes the little investor is always supposed to make — like selling out at the bottom. They expect the fund to sell before the bottom. The trouble is, the fund manager is no better than anybody else in telling where the bottom will be. So he dumps stock before it dives another dozen points or so and then discovers that the bottom has just been reached.

According to this manager, shareholders will forgive the fund that does not rise as fast or far as the average, but they will not forgive the fund that suffers a sharper drop. He says:

"In the first case, they can shrug it off: 'O.K., so we make a little less.' But in the second case, it's their money that's going down the drain. They feel it deep in the belly and don't forget it."

Funds' fears of being left at the post were responsible for the largest advance in market history. This occurred on August 16, 1971, the first trading day after President Nixon's announcement that he was freezing wages and prices and changing tax rates to make American products more competitive with those produced abroad. Initial reaction to his speech was wildly bullish. Funds jumped in furiously to buy the shares of companies that presumably would bring them huge increases in profits. Demands for shares of major automobile companies — expected to be the prime beneficiaries of Nixon's program — were so great that for a day not enough sellers could be found. On a record-breaking volume of 31.73 million shares, the Dow-Jones industrial average of 30 leading stocks soared 32.93 points.

Tape-watchers shudder to recall what happens when funds dump their stock at once. In the 1966 market drop, dozens of glamour stocks — particular favorites of investment managers — plunged like lead balloons, and portfolio managers feared a replay of 1929. Some threw huge blocks on the open market and seemed willing to take any price. The glamour stock of glamour stocks, Xerox, pushed by funds to a high of 267½ at the beginning of the year, was dumped in wave after wave until it dropped to 125¼ in October. Fairchild Camera — another darling of the institutions — was battered from 216 to 96. During the year almost 15 million Fairchild shares changed hands, 4 times the number outstanding and 16 times the usual turnover for New York Exchange stocks. News of a slight earnings dip caused fund managers to dump Motorola in waves. Earlier they had paid as much as $233 a share. Now they ditched it for as little as $89. "Panic — sheer panic" is the way one broker described the action.

The sequel to this exercise in mass hysteria also is noteworthy. In the fall of 1966 the market turned, and prices shot up. Xerox, Fairchild, Motorola, and other glamour stocks showed up more often on the ticker — a definite indication of institutional buying. The "professionals" who had hysterically sold out a few months before rushed back to buy at a 50 percent higher price.

Critics assert that funds that jump in and out of stocks for short-term gains have a harmful effect on the "social conscience" of business. As Roy A. Schotland, assistant dean of Georgetown University's Law School, remarked: "The in-and-out funds have had such an impact on the point of view of the operating companies [in which they invest] that the companies have dropped the longer view in the interests of immediate profits." Accordingly, companies under this pressure will not undertake such projects as pollution control or the training of minority-group workers because the costs would diminish their profits and, therefore, their company's popularity with the fund managers.

In Schotland's opinion, funds that engaged in too much short-term trading should be penalized. "We ought to limit the turnover," he says. "I don't mean to bar jumping in and out; I mean we should put a price on it. If you go into a stock, you ought to go in for fundamental reasons. If something changes your mind, you should get out free if your turnover rate is low. If it's high, you should pay a considerable price."[10]

The Wayward Go-Gos

In a 1968 address before a conference sponsored by *Institutional Investor* magazine, Manuel Cohen of the SEC accused certain money managers of catering to, and even whetting the speculative appetites of, the public. "More investors are apparently looking for dramatic short-term growth, high risk, leverage — in short, they are seeking to live dangerously — and many are doing it through the medium of institutions. I might add that there appears to be no shortage of institutional managers who are prepared to satisfy, and in many cases to foster, that demand."

According to Cohen, this "vicarious speculation" by investors who have turned their money over to professional managers contains the seeds of two grave dangers. "The disillusionment of investors who suffer substantial losses most likely will be turned against the people they consider responsible: the institutional managers. And this in turn could result in a corresponding loss of public confidence in securities markets in general."[11]

As far back as 1967 the threats that rampaging fund speculation posed for the welfare of the stock market were decried by William McChesney Martin, chairman of the board of governors of the Federal Reserve System. In a speech observing the 175th anniversary of the New York Stock Exchange, he declared:

> Some institutional investors are creating a new problem which poses a potentially more serious risk to the future well-being of stock markets. Increasingly, managers of mutual funds and portfolio and pension fund administrators are measuring their success in terms of relatively short-term market performance. In effect they set a target on a growth stock, attain that target, unload, and then seek other opportunities for quick capital gains.
>
> Given the large buying power of their institutions, there is an obvious risk that speculative in-and-out trading of this type may virtually corner the market in individual stocks. And in any event, activity of this kind tends to create undesirably volatile price fluctuations. I find this trend disquieting.
>
> However laudable the intent may be, it seems to me that practices of this nature contain poisonous qualities reminiscent in some respects of the old pool operations of the 1920s. I suggest that the Stock Exchange watch these activities carefully and make certain that this new cult of short-run market performance does not once again result in a tarnishing of Stock Exchange wares.[12]

But these words fell on deaf ears. While the Exchange looked on complacently, the go-go funds actually stepped up the speculative fever, which culminated in the crash of 1969 and early 1970. They turned on the heat again in 1971.

Fund critics allege that portfolio managers invest in thin stocks with the intention of pushing up their price and thus inflating their asset value per share. Thomas J. Holt, director of an investment advisory service, made this accusation in the fall of 1971 when several American Exchange issues rose strongly, and many New York Exchange stocks faltered. According to Holt:

"Many funds want to create good performance records so that they can rank high at the end of this year." He stated further:

> That's the way to attract new shareholders. These funds may have decided to sell off high-priced popular issues and use the proceeds to zero in on thinner issues with reasonably good earning performance and stock market grow power.

Heavy selling of such high-priced stocks as Polaroid, Disney, Avon, and Bausch & Lomb has depressed their value somewhat. But the funds are willing to accept a light beating on these stocks for the chance of sharp percentage gains on the Amex [American Exchange]. We don't know how long they'll keep up this buying, but when they finally turn around and sell the Amex stocks, heaven help the working girl.[13]

Wall Streeters speak of the fund manager who thought he saw a great chance for growth in a little electronic company with 150,000 shares in public hands. He bought a few hundred shares at 6, and a few hours later he discovered that the bid price had risen to 6½. He bought 300 more at that price, 200 more at 7, and 400 more at 8. The stock kept rising, and he kept buying. After he had accumulated 5,000 shares, and the price had risen to 17, he decided the stock was now "fully priced": the time had come to take his profits. He instructed his broker to sell 500 shares. Two hours later the broker reported that he had sold 200 shares at 16, 100 at 15, 100 at 14, and another 100 at 13. The stock that the fund manager had pushed up he now pushed down.

In this and many other instances, the fund's own buying power inflated the price of the stock. As long as it kept buying, it could show a "profit" on shares bought previously. But such a profit can be realized only if someone will take the shares off the holder's hands. In all too many cases, when the fund tries to sell its shares in infrequently traded over-the-counter issues, no one is there to buy them.

Whether real or imagined, the need to perform gives rise to various other practices. "Where once mutual fund portfolios were managed by seasoned investment committees, now they are more frequently run by a single portfolio manager," Norman F. Dacey charged in testimony before a congressional committee in 1969. Dacey went on to say:

Where the investment committee of yesterday had a field staff, the "new day" portfolio managers have broker friends who tip them off to situations, to "deals." The portfolio manager himself has no time to investigate each investment suggested to him, and so he comes to rely upon brokers and other "finders" whose standing with the portfolio manager is assured solely by the number of profitable deals they have brought to the portfolio manager in the past.

These are not the high standards of investment management which the industry describes so fulsomely in its sales literature. The adherents of this performance cult are simply playing the market with other people's financial security, with very little restraint imposed by law or by the regulatory authorities.

The new breed of portfolio managers loads his fund with convertible securities which everybody knows will never be converted. He buys a $1,000 debenture convertible into 100 shares of the issuer's common stock and thereafter has the best of two worlds. If the stock rises, he carries the debentures in his valuation sheet at 100 times the current market price of a share of the stock. If the stock falls, he carries the debenture at his cost price. Since in many cases he owns the only debentures outstanding, they are not traded and the price of his debenture holdings cannot fall in the market. He has no intention of trading them, for he would lose his valuation option.

In fact, Dacey said that he knew of two "ironclad agreements" between issuer and fund buyer to assure that the debentures would never be presented for conversion. "Raising money through this device is very desirable from the standpoint of the issuer," he declared. He said further:

> Only a small amount of stock is involved in the corporation's capitalization; the rest is debt certificates. The holders of the stock are thus enabled to retain control of the company. Of course, if the debentures were presented for conversion, the issuance of new common shares would water the company's stock and seriously undermine its value per share.
>
> In effect, then, when the mutual fund carries the debenture at a price based upon the market value of the stock, that valuation is a false one which could never be realized. If they did convert, the actual price of the stock would tumble. What we have, then, in the portfolios of countless mutual funds are billions of dollars of securities carried at a fictitious value — convertible securities which will never be converted. These contrived profits make no contribution to our economy. As with all phony investment values, someone must be hurt in the end.[14]

Fund managers themselves are acerbic critics of the practices of other funds. According to David L. Babson, president of

David L. Babson and Company, a Boston investment management firm, "Investment performance" is simply a euphemism for "a national crap game." At a 1968 conference of 1,300 institutional investors, he stated that money managers are:

> . . . responsible indirectly, if not directly, for the speculative orgy sweeping the country, particularly among unknowledgeable investors, and which is certain to bring financial loss to hundreds of thousands of people.
>
> When, on the average, mutual funds churn their holdings at an annual clip of 40 percent — when some turn them over completely in a quarter — can anyone seriously believe this is investing? In plain language the securities markets are being turned into a gigantic parimutuel operation. Yet here we — hundreds of experienced and responsible portfolio managers — are euphemistically discussing what's going on as "investment performance."[15]

Accusations that fund managers play games with restricted securities (so-called letter stock) have also been made. This is stock the fund has purchased from an issuer in a private agreement; such a procedure permits the issuer to bypass a ruling that stock offered the public must be registered with the SEC. Generally, common shares or convertible issues bought this way are priced much below the price at which the issuer's comparable issues sell in the open market. In return for the discount, the buyer signs an investment letter promising to hold the stock for a specified period, usually two or three years.

In the years preceding the 1969–1970 crash, dozens of mutual funds put letter stock in their portfolios. Frequently the price paid was only 30, 40, or 50 percent of the price quoted for the same securities on national exchanges or in the over-the-counter market. For example, Value Line Development Corporation bought one block of securities at 10 percent of the quoted market price. Other funds immediately marked up the value of their shares to, or close to, the quoted market price, disregarding the fact that their shares were not salable and that if they were put up for sale in large quantities, the market price would immediately plummet.

Testimony before the House Committee on Interstate and Foreign Commerce produced these examples of the way letter stock was marked up to help Enterprise Fund report a 114 percent gain in its net assets for 1967 — a gain greater than that of any other publicly traded fund:

On March 27, 1967, the fund paid $316,000 for Bell Electronics' convertible debentures. Its March 31 report listed the value of those debentures at $444,744 — a gain of 40 percent in four days.

On May 1 the fund bought 100,000 shares of Texas American Oil Company at $5.52 per share. The fund's June 30 report upvalued the shares 38 percent, to $7.63 each.

On June 28 Enterprise paid $743,000 for 50,000 shares of Wellington Electronics and upvalued them to $1,263,938 in its June 30 report — an appreciation of 59 percent, a third of a million dollars, in 48 hours.

On December 22 the fund bought 80,000 shares of AITS for $2,081,000 and put a value of $2,718,000 on those shares in its December 31 report six business days later — an increase of 30.6 percent.

On December 22 Enterprise bought 21,000 shares of Larson Industries for $2,101,000 and valued them five days later at $2,473,000 — an 18 percent increase.[16]

Obsessed with the need to perform well and to put on the best face possible, funds have resorted increasingly to the practice of "window dressing." The following story is an example of the way window dressing operates.

In June and July of 1971 Ted Danbury, manager of the Alpha-Zeta All-Purpose Fund portfolio, became convinced that the market would turn down sharply. He thus sold large blocks of stock and increased cash holdings to 20 percent. If the market dropped as he expected, the shareholder report for the period ending September 30, 1971, would state that the fund fully anticipated the downturn and therefore shrewdly built up a large cash reserve to "await proper buying opportunities."

Danbury took his vacation in August. While he was blithely sailing around the Greek islands, the market suddenly turned and shot upward. By the time he got the news and raced back to Wall Street, the Dow-Jones Industrial Average had shot up 50 points: the bundle of General Motors he had unloaded at 75 was now 85; his 100,000 shares of Polaroid, sold at 78, was valued at 110; his Xerox, which he was relieved to sell out

at 86, was 118. Some stocks he had held in his portfolio —
gold mining shares that he had counted on as a supreme
inflation hedge — had dropped sharply. Clearly, Danbury's
record looked none too good. Shareholders who saw a quarterly
report bereft of winners and filled with losers might head for
the redemption window.

Danbury obviously had to make the report look sweeter.
First he had to invest the cash; shareholders must not discover
that he had been caught with egg on his face. Next, he must get
rid of his holdings in the big losers and buy some of the fast-
moving stocks; thus shareholders, running their eyes down the
list of the fund's investments, would note that he had brilliantly
bought into those companies that had achieved the sharpest
gains. Fortunately for Danbury, the report will show only the
number of shares held on September 30 and their current
market value: it will not tell when the shares were bought or
the price paid. The portfolio manager may have window-
dressed with a vengeance, but the report will not show it.
Unless the shareholder critically compares the rise or fall in
asset value per share since the last reporting period with
results for the Dow-Jones or other average, or for mutual funds
generally, the shareholder may believe that his fund's manager
indeed has a flair for picking the right stocks at the right
price and dumping the wrong ones when they begin to wane.

Another expedient measure that fund managers frequently
employ to keep the good will of their shareholders is to declare
capital gains dividends. Such dividends can be declared only if
the fund sells securities at a profit every year. However, once
a fund manager embarks upon such a program, the manager
sacrifices freedom of action. For the sake of a good image, the
manager must sell stocks that he or she might otherwise prefer
to hold. Such window dressing may cost the shareholders an
appreciation in asset values over the long run, and it may result
in additional brokerage expenses, which ultimately increase
the fund's cost of doing business.

Fear of the Redeemer

In *How to Buy Stocks* Louis Engel directs attention to a
situation of nightmarish potential:

In the structure of most mutual funds there is one contradiction that can spell trouble. As a general rule, the mutual funds are particularly popular at a time when the market is going up. That's when the shares can be sold most easily. And yet that is precisely the time when it is most difficult and most risky for the fund to invest the new money that comes flowing in.

Even more dangerous is the situation that might exist if the market went into a tailspin. That's the time when people who owned shares in a mutual fund would be most tempted to cash them in, for that is when they as individuals would be most likely to need their savings. And yet that is precisely the time when it would be most difficult for a mutual fund to redeem its shares, because to raise cash it would probably have to sell stocks from its portfolio. . . . If there were a heavy run on the trust, it would have to sell off sizable blocks of stock to raise cash and it might very well have to take a loss on those forced sales. Additionally, those very sales might further depress the market and make it even more awkward for the trust to meet the next round of redemptions.[17]

A run on the funds might cause the value of fund shares to drop even more sharply than the average price of all stocks listed on the national exchanges. The reason for this, as we have seen, is that funds tend to buy the same kinds of stocks: whereas 500 institutions may invest in Mobil Oil, only one or two will invest in Wiggs Department Stores or Fanny Farmer Candy Shops. When funds must sell their shares to meet redemptions, they will try to sell the same things, forcing down the price of their favored stocks and reducing still more the asset value per fund share. However, in a time of heavy buying, in a generally rising market, when more money goes into mutual funds than goes out, the tendency to chase the same stocks pushes the price of these issues up (and makes the funds look good by increasing the value of their existing holdings). Unfortunately, stock prices usually go down quicker and sharper than they rise. And though price increases of stocks heavily held by institutions have usually been relatively gentle and have occurred over a long period of time, the possibility that a drop could be rapid and violent definitely exists.

"The hell that would break loose if a lot of fund shareholders demanded money at once is something we worry about a lot," one fund manager confided to this author. "About the best we can do is to pray that it won't happen," he added.

Nevertheless, the fear of a run for cash affects fund investment strategy. To a certain extent, moreover, this strategy could bring on the cataclysm it seeks to prevent. For example, at high points, when investor sentiment is ebullient, funds invariably are close to fully invested; only about $5 out of every $100 is held out of the market to meet redemption needs. But in a down market, as the redemption threat increases, the funds sell off more stock and increase their cash holdings. At past bottoms cash reserves have been greatest. Thus far there has been no problem in paying off investors: the market has always turned around in time; fears of redemptions have abated; and the funds have reinvested their cash. However, some future combination of stronger redemption pressure than has yet been experienced and more feverish selling by funds to enlarge their cash reserves in order to offset any increase in redemptions might cause a catastrophic drop, from which recovery might be long and agonizing.

A possible sign of things to come occurred in the spring of 1971, when the value of the shares redeemed by shareholders exceeded the value of shares sold by the industry. The net redemptions, the first on record, occurred in May and July. By August, however, new purchases regained a slight edge over redemptions. Indicative of Wall Street's awareness of the potentially devastating effect of a weak fund industry, stock prices dropped sharply when the first redemption figures were announced. Many explanations were offered for the net redemptions: the decline in the number of salespeople pushing funds; the desire of investors to "get out even" when share prices recovered from their plunge in 1970; the fact that many shareholders, now at retirement age, were beginning to withdraw capital for living expenses.

Officials of the Investment Company Institute, the trade association representing the mutual fund industry, explained the net redemptions "in terms of cyclical experience." As an ICI representative saw it:

> Redemptions are highly correlated with stock prices. The drop in stock prices between early 1969 and Mid-1970 was accompanied

by a prolonged and sharp downturn in dollar redemptions. The improvement in stock prices in the fall of 1970 was accompanied by an upswing in redemptions. In short, redemptions postponed during the period of declining stock prices augmented the "normal flow" of redemptions. This boosted the dollar level in the second and third quarters of 1971.

The pattern of increased redemptions in a period of rising stock prices has been signaled before. According to a common theory, fund shareowners sit tight while the value of their investment drops; but when the market recovers, they decide to get out "even."

What distinguished 1971 from previous years was the fact that the sale of new shares was considerably below the "normal" trend line. As a result, not enough new money came in to offset the amounts paid out.

Although it may be a long time before the full import of the funds' 1971 performance is known, this much can be said: the 1971 experience (which continued into 1972) signifies that funds can be forced to pay out as well as to take in, that the fearful prospect of a massive liquidation cannot be dismissed too hastily.

7

No-Loads: Fund Form
of the Future?

You want to buy stocks or bonds but lack the confidence, ability, or inclination to make investment selections on your own; you lack enough money to hire an investment counselor to manage a portfolio. So you have decided that mutual funds offer the best investment vehicle available to you.

Yet you recoil from paying a broker's or salesperson's commission of $8.50 for every $100 you invest. Is there a way to gain the advantages that fund investment offers without incurring the disadvantage of a substantial sales commission? The answer is yes. Each year thousands of investors prove this by investing in no-load funds, which charge no sales commission and put every one of your investment dollars to work for you.

Without doubt, the no-load fund represents an idea whose time has come. *If* you want to buy fund shares, and *if* you are prepared to accept the responsibility of choosing a suitable fund independently, a no-load fund is definitely for you.

The growth of mutual funds, as we have observed, has been

147

the most spectacular investment event in this century. Similarly, the growth of no-load funds is likely to prove the most spectacular event in the history of the fund industry itself. Figures supplied by the No-Load Mutual Fund Association, an organization consisting of the major non-commission investment companies, makes this development unquestionably clear. Indeed, the growth in recent years has been so spectacular that many Wall Streeters believe that it is the fund form of the future and that commissions charged for the purchase of fund shares will become obsolete.

In 1965 the idea of inviting investors to buy fund shares without requiring them to pay sales commissions was relatively unknown. At that time there were fewer than 30 such funds in the entire country, with only 28,000 no-load shareholders and total assets of $250 million. At the end of 1967, 61 no-load funds were selling their shares to the public. These funds had 358,107 shareholders and total net assets of $2.49 billion. By the end of 1970 there were 137 funds, with 1,161,500 share-holders and total net assets of $4.10 billion.

Although 1971 was a difficult year for investment companies, no-load funds continued to grow at an impressive rate. At the end of 1971 their total net assets exceeded $5 billion, an annual increase of almost $1 billion. In part, this 25 percent jump in assets was added by the rise in share portfolio values during the year. But for the most part this increase in assets was due to the fact that 28 no-load funds were organized during the year, bringing the total to 165 at the end of 1971. At the start of that year there were 1.2 million shareholders in no-load funds; at the year's end there were 1.4 million.

Advantages of No-Loads

In addition to giving the investor a head start on performance by putting all of the money invested to work at once, no-load funds offer other advantages. The absence of sales commissions and, usually, of redemption fees permits buying and selling without penalty. Unlike the buyer of load shares, you are not locked in for the long term. You can sell your shares without penalty if the fund's performance disappoints you, if you think it has reached its profit limit, or if you think the entire market is due for a spill and you want to hold cash. No-load funds can even be traded for short-term swings, although the funds discourage in-and-outers.

"I've been in a load fund for three years and still haven't got back the money I paid in commissions," one investor told me. "I don't want to be locked in that way anymore. Now I won't buy anything but no-load shares. I hope I won't sell them for 20 years, but I don't want a sales commission to go down the drain if I do."

Because they deal directly with the investors, many no-load funds have developed shareholder-relations services superior to those of the typical load funds. In general, no-load literature is clear and complete, and the funds try to answer shareholder questions promptly and fully. In contrast, load funds frequently depend so heavily on salespeople that their direct communications with shareholders are deficient.

Representatives of the No-Load Mutual Fund Association argue that no-load funds are less likely than load funds to be forced to liquidate their securities to meet redemption payments during a time of plummeting stock prices. According to their argument, the fact that their shares are *bought* rather than *sold* by a salesperson insures that the no-load shareholder has a built-in loyalty that makes the shareholder more immune to impulses or panic selling. Hence no-load funds may have greater stability of sales and redemptions in times of stress.

To the criticism that "no-load funds managed by investment organizations are a side operation for these firms and do not receive full attention," the no-load defenders reply that the investment adviser who also manages a mutual fund will treat it as a showcase for investment acumen and expertise. Therefore the adviser is likely to give the fund more, rather than less, attention.

Although no-load funds impose no sales charge for the purchase of shares, some may make service charges of $5 or so for opening an account and of $1 every time additional shares are bought. They may also reserve the right to impose a redemption charge of perhaps 1 percent on the net assets. Funds that do not exercise the option to make this charge presumably would do so if faced with a wave of redemptions.

Is It True What Salespeople Say about No-Loads?

In order to sell their own wares investment company sales-people sometimes misrepresent the difference between their own load funds and no-load funds. They claim that although the no-load fund carries no initial commission, its management charges are so much higher than those for the load funds that they eat away the investor's profits. This is nonsense. The difference between load and no-load funds rests entirely upon how they are sold, not how they are managed. Differences in management charges are insignificant. In 1966 the management cost (expense ratio) of all no-load funds with assets exceeding $1 million amounted to .82 percent. The cost of comparable load funds was .76 percent — six-tenths of a cent less on every $100 managed.[1]

A salesperson told a customer in Rye, New York, "No broker would touch a no-load fund, and that ought to convince you something's wrong with them." Of course, most brokers will neither recommend nor sell a fund that offers them no com-mission. This says nothing about the quality of the merchandise: the fact that a Cadillac dealer will not sell a Lincoln hardly proves that one car is better than the other. (Some brokers *do* recommend no-load funds, however. They get their payoff in the form of commission business from the grateful investment company.)

The accusation that no-loads are "untouchables" has cropped up with variations all over the country. In Sarasota, Florida, a retired restaurant owner and long-time investor told me this tale: He had been approached by a young salesperson who obviously knew less about his product than did his prospect. The retiree said that he already held thousands of fund shares, all of them no-loads. The salesman shook his head sadly.

"You'll have a hard time finding a broker to sell them for you," the salesperson said. "I know it," the investor calmly replied. "But aren't you worried about it?" "Not one bit."

The salesperson left, thoroughly perplexed. Indicative of the poor training that many receive in preparation for advising the public, this one seemingly believed that the retiree had been victimized in an investment swindle. Actually, brokers will not redeem shares of load funds. However, the procedure involved in getting your money when you decide to sell your shares is the same for both types of funds: you submit your shares to the investment company by registered mail and state in writing that you wish to redeem them. Within a few days, you can expect a check for the full amount due based on the net value of the shares at the time they are received.

Some salespeople use a battery of disparaging remarks about no-load funds, depending upon their customers' ignorance of the subject. When a prospect asks why he should pay a commission for one fund when he can get another without charge, a salesperson may eye the prospect with a trace of scorn and reply:

> Mr. Smith, you certainly know that a lot of things that look like bargains aren't bargains when you get them home. Now, you always get pretty much what you pay for. Why do you think funds are any different?
>
> Why do you suppose these funds have to sell their shares cheaper? The reason, Mr. Smith, is *because they couldn't sell them any other way!*

Of course, this is a half-truth: the fact that funds have no-loads is their most attractive feature. If they were sold through salespeople, a higher charge would result.

When dealing with an obviously unsophisticated customer, a salesperson may also insinuate that the upkeep of no-load funds is higher. "It's like buying a used car," a factory worker was told. "You can get what looks like a bargain on a used car lot, but when you get it home — brother, that's when you start to pay through the nose. It's the same with funds. When you start adding up management fees, advisory fees, custodian fees, and redemption costs on some of these funds, there's not much left for the shareholders."

The salesperson neglected to tell the prospect that once the sales charge is out of the way, no-load and load funds have basically the same operating costs. It is true that some no-load funds run at higher costs than load funds, but equally truthful is the fact that some no-loads also have below-average operating costs.

Defenders of load funds often complain that they do the missionary work and make the converts, and the no-load funds come along to take up the collection. Many people were first sold on the idea of investing in mutual funds through direct-sales campaigns or the enormous propaganda effort underwritten by the fund industry. However, once sold on the idea in general, they shopped around and decided that no-load funds offered a better deal. This is the "American way." Load funds still have the opportunity to prove that the customer gets something worthwhile for the sales charge. The fact that they still outsell no-loads seems to indicate that they have convinced buyers that their role in facilitating the purchase of shares justifies the cost.

It seems fair to assume that the investor who spends time and energy in choosing a fund is entitled to a lower price than the one who has others do it, in the same way that the shopper who personally selects soap powder and corn flakes from the supermarket shelves expects a lower price than one who phones the store to have the goods delivered.

Do Load Funds Perform Better?

Some fund salespeople imply that no-load funds do not perform as well as their commission-charging brethren. Such a claim is unjustified. After an exhaustive study of open-end investment companies the SEC concluded: "There is no appreciable difference between the performance of funds which charge sales loads and those which do not."[2]

To determine which form of fund is more advantageous for investors, *FundScope* magazine made an extensive study in 1971 of the records of 439 open-end investment companies: 355, or 81 percent, which charged sales commissions, and 84, or 19 percent, which did not. It compared results in relation to three investment objectives: namely, capital appreciation, income, and capital preservation. Results were measured for different market environments — periods of rising market prices and periods of declining prices. Current yields, the amounts paid to shareholders in the form of cash dividends, also were compared.

A comparison of 10-year capital growth (from January 1,

1960, to December 31, 1969) for load and no-load funds showed that the best performer was a load fund and that of the 5 top funds, 4 charged sales commissions, and 1 did not. Of the top 10 percent of funds that experienced the greatest increase in asset value per share, 14 were load funds, and 3 were no-load — a percentage roughly in line with the proportion of funds represented. Among the 10 percent of funds with the lowest appreciation, 16 were load funds; only 1 was a no-load. Here the *type* of fund was considered more significant: the three poorest performers were bond and preferred stock funds.

A comparison of cash dividends paid during the 10-year period shows the top 10 percent of the best dividend payers included 2 no-load and 14 funds that charged a sales commission of 8 percent or higher. Of 22 no-load funds 10 years old or older, 9 were ranked above average for dividends paid, and 13 were below average.

Similar results (some no-loads above average and some below) appeared in all other comparisons made in the study. *Fund-Scope* thus concluded:

> There just is no correlation between results on the one hand and the load (or absence of load) on the other. There just is no relationship between what a fund "does" and what it charges you to do it. . . .
>
> Some no-loads are among the best performers, and some are among the worst performers; some load funds are among the best performers, including those that charge the highest sales commission, and some load funds are among the worst performers, including those that charge the highest sales commission. If you are to select the best performers in line with your personal investment objective, you must start with performance first, then check the sales commission — and not the other way around.[3]

A test of the performance of no-load funds as a group versus load funds as a group was made in 1971 by Growth Fund Guide, an advisory service of San Clemente, California. The service examined figures for all funds generally available for sale during the past 21 years, from 1950 to 1971. Figures for the 1950–1959 period took all dividends in cash. In the figures for the 1960–1970 period income dividends were added, and capital gains distributions were reinvested. This study showed that

A TWENTY-ONE YEAR PERFORMANCE ANALYSIS — LOAD VS. NO-LOAD FUNDS

DEC. 31ST	No-Load Funds				Load Funds				5% Interest Account Compounded Annually
	VALUE OF INVESTMENT	ANNUAL % CHANGE	GAIN	LOSS	VALUE OF INVESTMENT	ANNUAL % CHANGE	GAIN	LOSS	VALUE OF DEPOSIT
1949	$ 10,000.00				$ 9,150.00*				$10,000.00
1950	$ 12,040.00	+20.4%	$ 2,040.00		$ 11,172.15	+22.1%	$ 2,022.15		$10,500.00
1951	$ 14,159.04	+17.6%	$ 2,119.04		$ 12,713.91	+13.8%	$ 1,541.76		$11,025.00
1952	$ 15,518.31	+ 9.6%	$ 1,359.27		$ 14,099.73	+10.9%	$ 1,385.82		$11,576.25
1953	$ 15,828.68	+ 2.0%	$ 310.37		$ 14,106.78	+ .05%	$ 7.05		$12,155.06
1954	$ 22,476.73	+42.0%	$ 6,648.05		$ 19,876.45	+40.9%	$ 5,769.67		$12,762.81
1955	$ 26,634.93	+18.5%	$ 4,158.20		$ 23,255.45	+17.0%	$ 3,379.00		$13,400.95
1956	$ 28,978.80	+ 8.8%	$ 2,343.87		$ 24,813.56	+ 6.7%	$ 1,558.11		$14,071.00
1957	$ 26,863.35	− 7.3%		$ 2,115.45	$ 22,381.83	− 9.8%		$ 2,431.73	$14,774.55
1958	$ 37,340.06	+39.0%	$ 10,476.71		$ 30,797.40	+37.6%	$ 8,415.57		$15,513.28
1959	$ 42,605.01	+14.1%	$ 5,264.95		$ 34,154.32	+10.9%	$ 3,356.92		$16,288.94
1960	$ 44,224.00	+ 3.8%	$ 1,618.99		$ 35,247.26	+ 3.2%	$ 1,092.94		$17,103.39
1961	$ 55,058.88	+24.5%	$ 10,834.88		$ 44,376.30	+25.9%	$ 9,129.04		$17,958.56
1962	$ 47,515.81	−13.7%		$ 7,543.07	$ 39,051.14	−12.0%		$ 5,325.16	$18,856.49
1963	$ 56,306.23	+18.5%	$ 8,790.42		$ 45,963.19	+17.7%	$ 6,912.05		$19,799.31
1964	$ 63,457.12	+12.7%	$ 7,150.89		$ 52,030.33	+13.2%	$ 6,067.14		$20,789.28
1965	$ 77,417.69	+22.0%	$ 13,960.57		$ 63,008.73	+21.1%	$ 10,978.40		$21,828.74
1966	$ 75,172.58	− 2.9%		$ 2,245.11	$ 59,606.26	− 5.4%		$ 3,402.47	$22,920.18
1967	$100,781.26	+34.0%	$ 25,558.68		$ 80,706.88	+35.4%	$ 21,100.62		$24,066.19
1968	$123,194.33	+22.3%	$ 22,463.07		$ 94,023.51	+16.5%	$ 13,316.63		$25,269.50
1969	$107,179.07	−13.0%		$16,015.26	$ 80,390.10	−14.5%		$13,633.41	$26,532.98
1970	$ 96,246.80	−10.2%		$10,932.27	$ 70,502.12	−12.3%		$ 9,887.98	$27,859.63
			$125,097.96	$38,851.16			$ 96,032.87	$34,680.75	

$ 96,246.80
− 10,000.00 Investment
$ 86,246.80 TOTAL GAIN

$ 70,502.12
− 9,150.00 Investment
− 850.00 Load Costs
$ 60,502.12 TOTAL GAIN

Investment $ 27,859.63
− 10,000.00
TOTAL GAIN $ 17,859.63

(*) $10,000 Investment minus 8.5% Load Costs   [Source: Growth Fund Research, Inc.]

$10,000 invested in the average no-load fund on December 31, 1949, would have grown to $96,246.80 by the last day of 1970. The investor with $10,000 on the last day of 1949 who invested in the average load fund would have a portfolio worth $70,502.12 in 1970. The preceding table gives the year-by-year figures.

William H. Rouleau, vice-president of Growth Fund Guide, attributed the superior performance on the no-loads to the absence of a sales charge. "Even if your position is that there is no difference between no-load and load funds and that both will perform about the same, all other conditions being equal, the fact that no-loads generally cost 9.3 percent less to buy makes them more desirable," he says. And again: "Over a period of years, the compounding of 9.3 percent of the original investment can be an eye-opener. In our study the amount saved on the sales charge grew to over $8,000."

Another reason why no-loads performed better, Rouleau believes, is that a higher percentage were growth-oriented. Since the period studied was one of generally rising markets, growth funds — load and no-load — increased their assets more than did their conservative counterparts. (In mediocre or declining markets, of course, growth funds may perform worse than other kinds.)

No-load funds try harder than load funds for performance, in Rouleau's opinion. "No-load funds sell their shares through advertisements in the printed media and by word of mouth rather than through a sales organization," he says. "Hence there seems to be an extra added incentive to turn in a good record. Good performance will quickly acquaint the investing public with a no-load fund and draw buyers to it."

The Do-It-Yourself Requirement

The major problem confronting you, of course, is that you must investigate and select a no-load fund yourself. Since no commission is involved, brokers as a rule are not interested in discussing such funds with you, much less going to the trouble of finding the one most suitable for your purposes.

Selecting a no-load fund is not that difficult, however. The Appendix of this book lists organizations that provide basic information on the backgrounds of such funds, their performance and objectives, as well as the names and addresses of funds to contact for more detailed information. You can also obtain information on no-load funds from the No-Load Mutual Fund Association, 375 Park Avenue, New York 10022.

It is important to remember that whether you buy a load or no-load fund, you have to do some investigating on your own to insure that you get what you want. You must be on your guard constantly. It generally is folly to buy shares of any kind simply because someone in the business tries to sell them to you. At the very least you should investigate the adviser to make sure that the person is honest and reliable. Since it is prudent to conduct a personal investigation whether you buy load or no-load shares, it also makes sense to pocket for yourself the substantial commission you otherwise would pay another.

There are persons in the investment business who would conscientiously try to find the fund that suits your objectives most perfectly and that performs reasonably well. But such persons are hard to find. If you find one, consider the necessary fees worthwhile.

Of course, managers of no-load funds are not in business to help you save your money. They operate such funds usually because they have reached a hard-headed decision that they can earn greater profits by doing so. Remember, fund managers get none of the sales commissions that are charged buyers of load funds. These sales charges are distributed to the underwriters and sales organizations that distribute the shares. The fund managers benefit from having their shares sold aggressively, for as the total assets under their management increase, so their fees proportionately increase. Fund organizers therefore must decide whether they can build assets faster by setting up a sales organization or by appealing to bargain hunters who want to bypass the commission structure.

The annual earnings of a successful no-load operation are indeed impressive. The T. Rowe Price organization of Baltimore, largest of the no-load managers, is estimated to earn some $2.8 million a year in advisory fees from its Growth Stock, New Horizons, and New Era funds.

For brokerage houses the prospect of a captive no-load fund is especially appealing. The broker then gets not only the management fees but (since the possibility that other brokers will sell the shares is written off) the fund's brokerage commissions. The experience of Lehman Brothers, a New York Stock Exchange firm, illustrates this fact. For years Lehman operated the One William Street Fund as a load fund, and, largely to induce other brokers to sell its shares, it said it would take none of the fund's brokerage business for itself. By 1964 Lehman discovered that these lost brokerage commissions were greater than the management fees produced through the efforts of other brokerage houses. It thus turned One William Street into a no-load fund and began handling its brokerage business as well.

No-load funds tend to attract large investors because savings on sales commissions become greater as the size of the purchase increases. For example, on an investment of $10,000 you can save $850 in sales fees by buying a no-load fund instead of one sold to you. A saving of this size should more than compensate for the trouble that investing in a no-load involves. That is, you will be confronted with the necessity of doing your own research — of consulting guidebooks and writing for prospectuses to determine which fund's investment objectives best match your own, of choosing the fund with the most appealing record and prospects, and of filling out and mailing the necessary forms.

If you have already bought load fund shares, there is no point in redeeming them for no-load shares. The commission you have paid is gone. You cannot get it back. If your load fund performs as well as a no-load fund, your gains from now on will be the same in either.

Nor is there any point in buying no-load shares simply because you save a sales charge. A no-load that performs poorly may do less for you than one in which you pay the standard commission. Because of the sales spread, moreover, a no-load fund can earn less year after year than a load fund and still enable you to finish ahead in the long run.

The Key Question

When, finally, a choice must be made between the load and no-load concepts, the key question is whether the services a load fund salesperson performs for you are worth the commission charged for them. Load funds naturally claim that you get value for your money; no-load funds say you don't.

"For the most part," says a representative of the no-load industry, "a mutual fund salesman is not qualified as an investment adviser or counselor. For investment advice, the investor should consult a qualified and registered investment adviser, his own banker or securities broker."

That advice is not entirely sound. Your best source of advice is someone who does not stand to profit from the advice given. Investment advisers have been known to discourage investments in mutual funds because they themselves want to manage the money involved. Securities brokers also have their own product to sell, and some bankers asked to recommend mutual funds may well introduce the questioner to their own trust departments. You must choose your adviser to make certain you will get objective guidance, or (and this is preferable in many cases) you must bite the bullet and make the decision for yourself.

Ultimately, your primary concern should be what you get for your money. Will you have more to show ten years from now from investment in a no-load fund than in a load fund? Because none of your money goes for sales commissions, you can start the race with a greater amount actually invested in no-load shares. But if its performance over the years is poor or if its income is eaten up by high advisory fees and operating costs, the fact that it was a "bargain" will not comfort you. If all other things are equal, the noncommission fund is naturally a better bet to finish the race first than the one that starts with a load on its back. But all other things are rarely equal, and even after deductions are made for sales charges, some load funds are more advantageous over the long run than some no-loads.

8

Before You Buy Shares
in Any Fund

To achieve satisfactory results from a fund investment you cannot choose just "any" fund. Over the years some funds have done well for their investors; despite highly favorable market conditions during certain periods, some have done poorly. Nor can you take "any" salesperson's word that he or she has just the fund for you. The evidence is all too clear: you must check into the fund's record yourself, or if you lack the interest or inclination to make such an investigation, you must thoroughly examine the salesperson's credentials and credibility before acting on any advice.

What Does It Take to Choose a Fund?

To choose a fund you must prefer to have someone else handle your portfolio decisions. Obviously, if you believe that you can manage your own affairs more successfully — and are willing to expend the time and effort required — you probably are not psychologically prepared to invest all your assets into funds.

To manage your own money it is imperative that you possess much self-confidence. The investment advisory industry spends millions of dollars a year to spread the propaganda that only "professional managers" can do a good job of it. But as Gerald M. Loeb, the veteran analyst who has been called "Mr. Wall Street" by many admirers, has observed, "Competent investors will never be satisfied beating the averages as it were, by a few small percentage funds, even if the funds they bought could do it in 11 years out of 11. The investor who truly and substantially wants to do better than drift up and down with the crowd must do his own buying and selling and concentrate on his own selections."[1]

Nevertheless, if you opt for the diversification and management that investment companies offer, you must decide what type of fund best suits your circumstances and objectives. *You must also make certain basic premises about the course of stock and bond prices during the period you will be holding your shares.*

As was discussed in Chapter 2, there are more than a dozen different kinds of funds with conspicuous differences in objectives and methods of operation among the funds in each category. A choice must be made between striving for a high level of current income (with varying safety, depending upon the quality of the income-producing vehicles chosen) and striving for capital gains (also with varying risks). As a rule, you cannot put your money into an ultrasafe place and expect either a high return or prospects for high capital gains, let alone both.

In general, the widow seeking a dependable monthly check to cover her living expenses might be best accommodated by putting her money into high-quality bonds; she should select a fund specializing in such investments. The young couple, with more than enough current income, generally prefers investments that pay little or no dividends now but offer prospects for capital gains. A growth fund that seeks out small companies with good chances for expansion might suit them best. The middle-aged couple, neither income- nor risk-oriented to the same extent as the old or young, might prefer a balanced fund, which provides some income and some hopes of capital gains but also takes some risks. In short, the fund you choose should be tailored to your own needs and wishes.

Assume that you want to live from the income on your assets for the rest of your life. If you buy shares in a bond fund, its present return — helped by occasional dips into your capital — might enable you to get by at today's prices. But can you be confident that long-extended inflation of 4 percent or more a year will not slash into your purchasing power? Therefore, before you invest in a bond fund, particularly one with a sales charge that tends to lock you in for years, you must decide that inflation will be slowed if not stopped and that the dollars you draw in interest 15 years from now will resemble somewhat those you have today.

Any long-term commitments in common stock funds should be based on the premise that stock prices will appreciate faster than, for example, money in a savings account or bond portfolio. In the past mutual funds on average have done no better than the averages of common stocks themselves. It is the rare fund whose asset value per share will grow spectacularly while stock prices in general rise little or not at all. Rarer still is the fund the value per share of which will not drop when market averages drop. In point of fact, to invest in a common stock mutual fund intent on capital gains is to be tied to the stock market itself. Before buying any such fund shares you should be convinced that over the long term the Dow-Jones Industrial Average of 30 stocks, Standard and Poor's composite index of 500 stocks, and the New York Stock Exchange average will show a better return than you could get elsewhere.

You are led to believe that *everybody* knows that "stock prices will rise over the long term," and "stocks are a hedge against inflation." That is reason enough to be suspicious. Historically, forecasting has erred in the assumption that the future repeats the past. Indeed the idea that a trend in motion will indefinitely continue in motion probably leads more investors astray than any other. Hence they fail to sell at the top of a bull movement and fail to buy at the bottom of a bear movement. This does not mean that you can automatically profit by going against the crowd. What "everybody knows" is incorrect so often that it ought not to be taken for granted.

Will Stock Prices Go Up and Up and Up?

Some knowledgeable analysts believe that the "glory days"

of common stocks are over, at least for the near future. It is almost certain that it will be difficult for stockholders of the 1970s to do as well as those of the 1960s. In an analysis ominously entitled "A Bad New Era for Common Stocks," *Fortune* observed in October, 1971: "We are . . . in fact, we have been for some time . . . in a new era on Wall Street; the casino has changed the rules. Under the new rules players still run large risks, but payoffs to the winners are relatively meager. . . . In an important sense, stocks have 'had it.'"

Fortune also cited the likelihood of continued inflation, which would keep interest rates high and make bonds competitively attractive; the likelihood of huge stock offerings by large corporations, increasing the supply of shares competing for investors' funds; and the probability that pension fund managers will not buy as much common stock in the future as they have in the recent past.[2]

Half a dozen factors support *Fortune*'s predictions. In general, common stock prices are related to a company's earnings prospects. The great high fliers of history have been corporations with rapidly rising profits and strong prospects for the future. As a result of President Nixon's price freeze in August, 1971, Washington began to exercise stronger controls over the corporation's ability to increase prices and, therefore, profits. Many observers feel that these controls will not be removed for years, if ever.

Inasmuch as most voters are consumers first and stockholders second, if at all, many astute politicians will find it advantageous to keep prices down. Pressures on profits may also arise from the higher taxes needed to rebuild the cities, to provide more social services (welfare, health care, etc.), and to fight pollution. Some believe that the cost of clearing the air and cleansing the waterways alone could eliminate the earnings of most large corporations. Moreover, the overall mood of the young — the voters who will determine governmental policy in coming years — is distinctly anticorporate. If the free enterprise system survives, it is argued, America's corporations will find it more difficult than ever to get their profits past the tax collector and into the hands of their stockholders.

Although some fund representatives claim that common

stock investments provide a reliable hedge against inflation, the record proves the contrary. In fact, since 1950 stock prices have risen in periods of low inflation — relative stability by modern standards — but have declined in more inflationary periods. From 1952 to 1955, the annual inflation rate amounted to only 1.4 percent on the average; the Dow-Jones index of 30 industrial stocks rose 16.1 percent. In 1956 and 1957 inflation intensified to a 3.8 percent annual rate; the Dow-Jones average declined 5.3 percent. Comparative stability was restored from 1958 to 1965, when the inflation rate was a relatively modest 1.6 percent annually; stock prices rose 10.5 percent. From 1966 to 1970 inflation rose to 4.3 percent a year; stock prices dropped 3.5 percent.[3] Furthermore, few economists predict an inflation rate of lower than 3 percent for the 1970s.

Complete agreement with all these portents of doom is not required in order to recognize that it will be harder to make stock market profits in the future. The records of gains rolled up by mutual funds in the 1950s and 1960s are not likely to be duplicated. Accordingly, the idea circulated by fund defenders that they have found an automatic way to make people rich merits serious questioning.

Numerous studies of fund performance indicate that it closely resembles that of the stock market as a whole. If the market rises, the value of your fund shares probably will rise. If the market falls, the value of your own holdings will drop. By their nature, funds as a group are locked into the market and usually have 90 percent or more of their assets invested in it. (As a group, they probably could not get the bulk of their assets out of the market even if they saw a severe slump coming. In fact, the mass selling by the funds would precipitate the very market they foresaw — thus cutting the value of the shares remaining in their portfolios.)

The record shows quite plainly that you cannot count on a fund to choose stocks that will go up while the market turns down; or, in Wall Street's timeworn analogy, "When the police raid a bawdy house, they take all the girls." In the bear market of 1969-1970 all common stock funds suffered; many go-go performance outfits suffered far more drastic reverses than did the averages of all stocks taken together.

The important question, therefore, is this: will stock prices rise as they have in the past?

Stockholders in recent decades have done better than average. Mutual funds have achieved better results than their shareholders could have obtained by keeping their money in savings accounts or reasonably safe bonds. The Investment Company Institute, the national association of the fund industry, points out that a $10,000 investment in an average mutual fund in 1950 would have earned $70,237 in two decades. But $10,000 put in a savings account or bonds, paying 5 percent interest compounded annually, would have earned $17,863, only one-quarter as much.

Fund salespeople like to extrapolate these figures to show what your investment will do if future performance equals that of the past. Thus they can project, for example, that the couple in their late twenties who invest only $100 a month in fund shares will — on the basis of past performance — be millionaires when they are sixty.

The assumption that mutual funds' future performance will parallel the past contains serious flaws, however. If stock prices have risen solely because corporate earnings have risen in the same proportion, the price increase would be soundly based. But the rise in stock prices since 1950 is only partly related to increased earnings. To a larger extent, today's stock prices are higher because stockholders have almost doubled the amount that they will pay for each dollar's worth of earnings.

As of January 1, 1950, the Dow-Jones Industrial Average of 30 industrial stocks was 200.13. Earnings of the stocks in the index for the preceding 12 months were $23.54. The price-earnings ratio (the number of times the price of the stock exceeded its earnings) was 8.5. That is, investors were willing to pay $8.50 for each dollar of earnings. As of January 1, 1972, the Dow-Jones industrial index was 890.20; earnings for the preceding 12 months were $53.30; and the price-earnings ratio was 16.7. Investors were now willing to pay $16.70 for each dollar of earnings.

During the 22-year period annual earnings of the corporations in the index increased 2.26 times. But stock prices went up 4.45 times — twice as fast. Were it not for the willingness of investors to pay more for each dollar earned, the Dow-Jones index would have stood at only 453 at the beginning of 1972.

The assumption that stock prices will advance at the same rate in the next 20 years as in the past means, in short, that earnings and the price-earnings ratio will double, that the Dow-Jones average will earn $106 and that investors will pay 33 times earnings. If earnings increase at a lower rate, the price-earnings ratio will increase at a higher one; if the rate of gain of the price-earnings falters, the earnings increase will be greater.

If investors paid 33 times such earnings, they would receive an earnings return (not a dividend return) of only 3 percent a year on their money. In the past, investors always demanded a greater dividend return on common stock than on corporate bonds. As of the end of 1971, however, the interest paid on top quality AAA bonds (considered safe as regards both principal and interest) was more than double the dividends paid on the 30 stocks making up the Dow-Jones Industrial Average. At that time, industrial bonds in the Dow-Jones Bond Average were also earning 22 percent more in cash interest than industrial stocks in the average earned.

Perhaps investor thinking concerning risks and rewards in common stocks and bonds has undergone a permanent change. However, if interest rates and corporate profit growth continue at present levels, price-earnings ratios must continue to climb to unrealistic heights in order for stock prices to rise as they have in the past.

In any event, if you believe that in the long run stock prices will continue to rise, you might do well to invest in stocks directly rather than to have a fund do it for you.

Because individual investors tend to "buy and hold," their long-term performance record over a period of rising stock prices is impressive indeed. As the SEC Institutional Investor Study Report concluded:

> Individuals have held around 70 percent of outstanding corporate stock since the late 1950s, even though they have been net sellers during much of that same period. These facts suggest that the securities which individuals have retained or purchased have appreciated more rapidly than have those which

were held or purchased by institutions. While such an investment strategy increases vulnerability to large losses in declining markets, it also leads to better than average gains during rising markets. Thus, individual direct investors have performed better than the market as a whole and better than institutions as a group on a total return basis over the rising market that characterizes most of the period.[4]

The Only Game in Town

Mutual fund investment may be the only feasible medium open to investors either uninterested in managing their own portfolios or convinced they have been edged out of the market. Indeed the brokerage business has done an extraordinarily effective job in discouraging small investors from buying stocks and bonds directly. Moreover, the extremely high commissions charged on small transactions, the extra cost per share charged the buyer, and the lower price received by the seller of less than 100 shares have effectively told the small investor that the stock exchange houses do not want the investor's business. If the investor does not back off because of the financial odds against him or her, the registered representative with whom the investor tries to place his "puny" order often will indicate plainly that the investor's business is unwanted. As a result, in 1971, odd-lot investors (who purchase less than 100 shares at a time) actually sold almost twice as many shares as they bought. They turned their stocks into cash and left the market.

For the latter, mutual funds provide a ready answer. Many funds, load and no-load, will open accounts if you have only $100 to invest and will accept orders of as little as $25 thereafter. These economic facts explain the attitude of one small investor who had only $500 but preferred to buy and sell securities on his own. He thus purchased shares in a no-load fund. "For people like me," he says, "it's the only game in town."

Before purchasing mutual fund shares remember that the wide variety of funds available means that many are completely inappropriate for you. As *Fortune* commented in April, 1969:

> We can certainly no longer take it for granted that the funds are appropriate vehicles for the small, cautious investors. In the past year or so there has been an extraordinary explosion of new

funds, most of them appealing to growth-oriented sophisticated investors, many of them avowedly speculative and proposing to deal, not only in stocks and bonds, but in commodities and warrants, to take short as well as long positions, and, following the lead of the voguish hedged funds, operating on margin (i.e., they will invest not only the funds generated by sales of shares but borrow funds as well). . . . The presumption that mutual funds were, as Professor Louis Loss of Harvard put it, "the poor man's investment counselors" . . . obviously needs a review.[5]

A second basic point is that a mutual fund should be a long-term commitment. In the case of a load fund, which charges up to an 8½ percent commission, some advisers say that you should be prepared to hold your shares at least ten years. (Based on the record, it will take a year before the shares appreciate enough to cover the commission you paid.) Of course, commissions are not charged on sales of no-load shares; and even if you sold your shares within a few months, you probably would not lose any money. Nevertheless, funds are generally considered long-term investment vehicles and should not be bought and sold in hopes of short-term profits. (If you could successfully call market turns, you could invest on your own, without a fund manager.)

Remember, you are buying fund shares that you will hold for a long time; therefore, you should investigate them thoroughly. "I tell my customers they may be holding these shares longer than they'll hold their husbands or wives," one fund broker told me. "So I advise them to investigate the fund shares thoroughly, as though it's a once-in-a-lifetime proposition."

The Story the Prospectus Tells

Before you buy shares in any fund, get its prospectus and read it. This is a printed document that describes the fund — its objectives and background — in detail. The law requires that a fund or its agent deliver a prospectus prior to the purchase of its shares. If the prospectus is not accurate, the fund's managers may find themselves in jail. The prospectus is probably the most objective statement about the fund that you can find anywhere. Nevertheless, a study by the Wharton School of Finance and Commerce revealed that 20 percent of the new purchasers of regular fund accounts and 10 percent of the contractual plan purchasers said that they did not receive a copy of the fund's prospectus before they bought. (A majority of those who did not get prospectuses were customers of member firms of the New York Stock Exchange.)[6]

Moreover, of those who receive a prospectus, only a small fraction take the trouble to read it. Although a prospectus is frequently written in lawyer's jargon, shocking facts often are laid bare, and deficiencies are revealed in stark prose that anyone can understand. The beauty of the prospectus is that it tells what the fund salesperson would not dream of revealing (or may not even know); if you buy the shares of a fund without reading and analyzing this document, you are to blame if your investments turn sour.*

Since mutual funds always offer their shares to the public, they are "constantly in registration." They must prepare a new prospectus every year for the examination of prospective shareholders.

First look in the prospectus for a statement of the fund's objectives, found on the front page. A more detailed discussion of what the fund intends to do and how it intends to do it generally can be found inside. These are *basic policies*, under which the fund has agreed to operate. A fund can change these policies only with its shareholders' approval. By reading this statement you can confirm whether or not the fund's objectives coincide with your own: if you seek a conservative fund to provide substantial dividends from fixed-income investments, you will not find appealing a statement that, "The fund seeks maximum capital gains and will take what it considers reasonable risks to obtain them."

The SEC requires that a fund also state its unusual char-acteristics and possible disadvantages on the first page of the prospectus. For example, on the cover of the prospectus for the First Spectrum Fund, a no-load trust organized primarily to invest in companies with a "social conscience," the reader is

---

* In effect, the prospectus is largely written by the SEC. This agency issues guidelines for funds with examples of "acceptable statements" covering all the factual material that must be included. The task of writing a suitable prospectus is thus simplified. It is almost a question of pasting the appropriate "acceptable statements" together in the prescribed order.

informed that, "The fund is newly-organized and has no operating history"; that "The investment adviser for the fund is also newly-organized and has had no previous experience in managing the assets of an investment company such as the fund"; and that, "The fund pays an advisory fee of approximately 1 percent per annum of the average value of its net assets. This fee is higher than that paid by many funds."

The prospectus must contain background information on the fund's officers and directors. Although funds are not legally required to provide information on their portfolio managers, many do, particularly those confident that the education and experience of their investment managers will withstand close scrutiny. If the prospectus does not disclose this information, ask the salesperson for it (if it is a load fund) or the company (if it is a no-load fund). Do not invest in any fund that does not reveal who makes its investment decisions.

Knowledge of the background of the fund's adviser or advisers can tell you much about it. The adviser should have been in the securities business long enough to have experienced at least several sharp bull and bear markets. The presence of such experience should safeguard against the "whiz kid" fund managers of 1967–1968, who, never having lived through a sharply breaking market, failed to protect their shareholders when it came.

An adviser should have a postgraduate degree (for example, at least a Master of Business Administration degree) from a reputable university or sufficient on-the-job training to make up for any lack of formal education. Of course, neither education nor experience guarantees an outstanding performance by the adviser. But it usually means that the adviser will not commit the most flagrant errors.

The best measure of an adviser is actual performance in both rising and falling markets. If a fund has had the same portfolio manager for 10 years or so, you can check on his actual accomplishments. Obviously, the longer the adviser has been with the fund, the easier it is to estimate probable future performance. But it is also important to know that the person is not so old that he or she might soon retire and be replaced by an unknown quantity.

If the adviser has been with the fund only a short time, it

might be prudent to ask additional questions. Have the fund's basic investment philosophies changed? If so, have past performance records become meaningless? Does the fund have trouble keeping its advisers? If so, this is not a good sign for shareholders. It indicates dissatisfaction or friction at the top — rarely a characteristic of a successful organization. Does the adviser have a record of moving from job to job? If so, you might have to withstand another change of direction in investment policy in a few years.

The prospectus must contain a separate section entitled "brokerage"; this discusses in a clear and concise way how buy and sell orders are placed. According to the official guidelines, this section should state whether it will be the company's policy to secure, "consistent with best execution," the highest possible prices on sales and the lowest possible prices on purchases of securities for the company's portfolio. If this will not be the fund's policy, the section should disclose the reason. This section should also indicate who is responsible for placing the company's brokerage business and commissions and what connection, if any, there may be between the fund's officers, directors, investment adviser or principal underwriter, and the broker-dealers who get the fund's commission business. This disclosure requirement has resulted in many a book being thrown at fund organizations — not because they set up cozy arrangements between advisers and brokers but because the prospectus did not reveal such arrangements.

Look for a description of any irregular investment techniques in which the fund may engage. If the company intends to sell securities short, the prospectus must explain the investment technique. It must explain what a short sale is; the risks, including timing, involved in short selling; the circumstances under which the company will sell short; the percentage of the value of the company's assets that will be deposited as collateral against short positions; and the impact that short sales may have on income taxes.

Also note the amount, if any, of restricted securities held by the fund. These securities are sold at prices below prevailing market levels; in return for this the buyer receives a letter stipulating that he or she will not sell the stock to the public for a specified period, which may be as long as three years. Before the shares are sold, a registration must be filed with the SEC, and it may be necessary to pay large sums to an underwriter to dispose of them to the public. Hence letter stock should be bought at a substantial discount from the present market price.

The presence of large amounts of letter stock in a fund's portfolio sharply limits its freedom to buy and sell other securities. The fact that sale of this stock is restricted may force the fund to sell its other stock to redeem fund shares presented by shareholders.

The prospectus will also provide:

1. *An explanation of the terms of the investment advisory contract.* This should disclose exactly how much the fund intends to pay its investment advisers and what services the payments will cover. Here it may be indicated that the managers of the investment advisory firm are also members of the fund's board of directors. Such a relationship may jeopardize the ability of the board of directors to assess objectively the performance of the advisers. As a result, the advisory firm may be retained no matter how poorly it performs for the shareholders.

2. *A breakdown of sales charges, including breakpoints at which lower commissions are charged.* The fund itself is not the recipient of the sales commission paid by the investor in a load fund. Rather, the commission goes to the sales force and to the underwriter, who — thanks to the short arm of coincidence — is often intimately related to the fund's adviser and its board of directors.

    Breakpoints at which sales charges decrease usually are at $25,000, $50,000, $100,000, etc. If you invest $1 million at one time, the charge may drop to 1 percent.

    Salespeople are supposed to alert their customers to the savings possible by buying at breakpoints, but as we noted earlier, some fail to do so through oversight, indifference, or greed. If you get close to a breakpoint (or intend to buy enough shares to entitle you to the lower breakpoint commission within 14 months), you should explore ways of taking advantage of this saving. Such methods include letters of intention, contractual plans, and even borrowing from a bank on a short-term basis. (These methods are discussed in greater detail below.)

3. *An indication of what the dividend distribution policy will be.* Under the Internal Revenue Code, a fund need pay no income tax if it distributes 90 percent of its gross income from dividends and interest to its shareholders. (This is an advantageous arrangement for investors. It avoids the double taxation that would result were the fund taxed on its income and shareholders taxed again on the dividends they received. The shareholders pay taxes at their individual tax rate, which, except for extremely upper-bracket taxpayers, is lower than the corporate rate.) Although funds are entitled to keep 10 percent of their net income free of tax, most of them distribute all of their net income to shareholders annually.

   Capital gains distributions represent profits realized in securities transactions. Generally these vary from year to year, depending upon the fund's success in choosing stocks that rise in price and upon the management's decision to nail down profits. The fund need not distribute such gains. It may choose to pay the tax at corporation rates; if these are higher than the shareholder's rates, the shareholder may file for a refund. (Some salespeople represent that the investor benefits from a provision taxing such distributions at capital gains rates even if the shares have been held less than the six months usually required for that lower rate. However, the investor already paid the tax when he or she purchased the fund's shares, for the net asset value reflects current market value.)

4. *A description of when the net asset values are determined.* Most funds compute the value of all their holdings twice each day the New York Exchange is open — at 1:00 P.M., three hours after the opening, and at 3:30 P.M., when the market closes. If your order is placed between 2:00 and 4:30 P.M., the 1:00 price is in effect; if placed between 4:30 P.M. and 2:00 P.M. the next day, the closing price

prevails. In this computation each portfolio security is valued at its latest reported sale price on a national exchange and at the mean between the bid and price asked if the security is sold over the counter. Where no market quotations are available, the securities are valued at "fair market value."

Shrewd investors or speculators theoretically can exploit the fact that fund prices remain in effect even after prices of their portfolio securities may have changed dramatically. Several times in recent years presidents have made announcements at night, which provoked sensational price rises the next morning. On the night of August 15, 1971, President Nixon announced an "economic game plan" to curb inflation, produce employment, and stem the outflow of dollars to other countries. The next day the stock market rose spectacularly. By noon the Dow-Jones Industrial Average had risen 33 points. The alert fund investor might have bought shares at that time at the prices set at the previous close. There may also be an interval between a sudden drop in stock prices and the corresponding markdown in the value of fund shares. During the interval the shareholder may sell at the previously prevailing higher price.

5. *A statement describing how the shares can be redeemed.* As we have noted, a mutual fund's distinguishing characteristic is its readiness to redeem shares upon demand. Before buying the shares you must learn whether the shares can be redeemed without cost to you. In most cases this is so. However, some no-load funds may make a redemption charge amounting to 1 percent of the net assets. Usually the shares must be delivered to the underwriters — those who sold the shares through dealers in the first place — or to the dealer from whom you bought them. If the shares are held by the fund, it may require a formal written request to itself or to the bank serving as its custodian.

6. *A statement concerning the fund's attitude toward social issues*: whether, before deciding to buy a corporation's

shares, it considers the corporation's record on pollution, employment of minority groups, and other national problems. Increasingly fund investment managers are using the power of their purse to get corporations to exercise more social responsibility: to avoid damage to the environment, to end racial discrimination, and to curb investments in countries with widely opposed internal policies, such as South Africa and Greece. You may or may not agree that funds should get involved in such matters, that it is possible for them to do good and perform well at the same time, and that profits should be made secondary to social considerations. These are matters you should resolve, for your attitude about them will help to determine which fund to select.

Study the Fund's Portfolio

Examine the fund's portfolio by consulting its most recent annual and quarterly reports. More than any sales literature, its list of holdings can tell you its investment philosophy, whether it is conservative or speculative. The fund heavily invested in giant corporations (General Motors, General Electric, International Business Machines) probably will not experience sharp price fluctuations. One whose assets are largely invested in companies completely unfamiliar to you is obviously more speculative. Its asset value may rise more sharply than the average in bull markets but may plummet like a dead bird when the market climate turns stormy.

Also note how much the fund's various investments have increased or decreased in value since it made them. These figures show the extent to which capital gains are a factor in the net assets; *these are capital gains upon which a tax must be paid*. When you buy shares in funds with large capital gains, you are "carrying water to another's elephant." When the fund sells such investments at a profit, you are responsible for the tax. In effect, therefore, you may be buying a tax liability.

On the other hand, a fund holding stocks with a market value less than the amount paid for them can gain a certain amount in its net asset value without incurring a tax liability.

It is important to avoid buying the shares of a fund with substantial capital gains *just before* it declares a "capital gains distribution" in any case, but doubly important if you buy shares in a load fund. Then you not only buy a tax, but you pay an added sales commission for the privilege of paying the tax. Here is how this hazard works.

Say that you receive a $5,000 Christmas bonus. You decide to salt it away in a mutual fund and consult a fund salesperson. According to the rules of the game, the salesperson should warn you not to buy when dividends are coming due, but he or she may neglect to do so.

On your $5,000 you face a sales charge of 8½ percent, or $425. Assume that the remaining $4,575 buys 366 shares at $12.50 per share. Soon thereafter the fund declares a dividend of $.40 from ordinary income and $1.00 from capital gains. After paying income taxes of 40 and 20 percent, respectively, you can put only $1.04 in your pocket. And each share is worth only $11.10 because the amount of the distributions has been deducted.

After sales commission and tax bites your $5,000 is worth only $4,444. You have $417.24 in cash and shares valued at $4,062.60 that cost you $556 to acquire. This amounts to a cost of almost 14 percent, and it may take you well over a year before you again have assets worth $5,000.

The prospectus and annual reports should indicate how much fund income is used for expenses and how much flows through to shareholders. The only way to interpret these ratios is to compare records of different funds. (Such comparisons are made by several fund-rating services, listed in the Appendix.)

The expense ratio relates the total costs of running the fund to its average net assets. These costs — for reports to shareholders, charges to transfer agents for redeeming fund shares, legal services, charges by banks that hold the securities in the fund's portfolio, and the like — ordinarily are lower for large funds than for small ones.

The income ratio demonstrates how much of the fund's intake (from dividends, interest, and realized capital gains) is consumed by operating costs. You must relate this ratio to the fund's investment objectives. For instance, if it aims at capital gains, its income from dividends will be low, and the income ratio, therefore, high. On the other hand, a fund specifically set up to produce income that has a high income ratio probably is not operating efficiently.

Ratios are much less significant than the fund's performance record. Since your primary interest is in the overall results of the fund, a high-expense fund with an outstanding profit record is obviously more desirable than one with low expenses but mediocre results.

Does Bigger Mean Better?

In choosing a fund remember that size is not necessarily a measure of quality. Performance records of the largest funds fail to demonstrate that they achieve more for their shareholders than do funds with smaller assets. As we have seen, mere size usually proves only that the fund has aggressive selling policies. Theoretically, large funds should bring you greater benefits; their size enables them to cut the per-share cost of custodial, stock transfer, dividend disbursing, printing, legal, and auditing expenses. The huge sums they receive in advisory fees should enable portfolio managers to investigate more thoroughly every company in which they invest, and buying and selling shares in large blocks should enable them to bargain for lower brokerage commissions.

Frequently, however, the advantages of size are offset by serious liabilities. Due to the fact that large funds must take large positions in each stock they hold, they often cannot take advantage of price movements. They often must pay more per share when they buy and accept less per share when they sell. Their size forces them to concentrate their investments in the largest corporations, which have often already experienced their greatest growth and are unlikely to be stand-out market performers.

Studies by investigators from the Wharton School of Finance, by members of the SEC staff, and by independent researchers found no evidence that performance of the largest funds was better than the average. The SEC staff examined the investment performance of 150 mutual funds for the 10-year period from 1956 to 1965. Records of individual funds were compared to the median (middle) performance record for all funds claiming similar investment objectives.

One part of the investigation focused on funds with net assets of $300 million or more at the end of the study. A majority of these large funds (18 out of 26) performed above average for the 10-year period. Significantly, the researchers found that funds that were smaller in 1956 had better performance than funds that were large to begin with. Thus 9 of the 11 funds with net assets below $100 million at the beginning of the period had above average performance, while only 2 of the 5 funds with more than $300 million in assets at the beginning of the period performed better than average.

Eight of the funds studied were the industry giants, with assets in 1965 of more than $1 billion each. Half of these 8 had below average performance for the 10-year period, and the four poorer performers were the largest of the large, with assets ranging from $1.8 to $3 billion. As SEC researchers concluded: "The performance of the largest funds on the whole has been no better than that of all funds in similar investment-objective categories. Although the largest funds have lower operating expense ratios, lower portfolio turnover rates and greater management resources, these funds have not had superior performance as would be expected."

Does this mean that smaller funds are better for you? The investigators also subclassified the smallest funds into three groups — those with assets below $1 million at the end of the period, those with $1 to $5 million, and those with $5 million and over. Only 5 of the 15 smallest funds achieved performance records above average. The funds that performed best grew out of the under $1 million group. Five of the 11 funds that increased assets above $1 million scored better than average, while none of the 4 funds that stayed very small managed to do so.[7]

These studies suggest that the best performers among the funds generally are those in the middle-asset category (above $10 million and below $300 million in assets). Funds in this bracket generate large enough advisory fees to attract competent portfolio managers, thus overcoming a major handicap of the smallest funds. They also do not suffer from elephantiasis, as do the largest ones.

Unfortunately, the evidence is not decisive. You cannot choose just any medium-sized fund and obtain superior results. Some of these have poorer records than some of the smallest and some of the largest funds. The implication is clear: you must examine each fund as a separate entity, comparing its performance with that of all other funds with the same objectives.

Although past performance is not an infallible guide, it serves as a good indicator of the general competence of a portfolio manager. However, if a fund's superior results depend upon one individual, the risk exists that if the investor leaves the fund, its performance will suffer. After the spectacular appreciation of Enterprise Fund assets in 1967 and 1968, thousands of investors bought its shares, hoping to benefit from the glow cast by portfolio manager Fred Carr. However, in 1969 Carr left the fund.

On the other hand, if a fund has a reasonably successful record over the years, one can assume that its chief officers know the type of expertise qualities required to be a good portfolio manager. Although the Fidelity Funds of Boston have had a succession of portfolio managers, they remain highly regarded on Wall Street because at their head is Edward Johnson. Johnson, considered one of the most knowledgeable in the business, could survive the loss of any portfolio manager.

There are great risks when investor speculation in a "hot" fund is motivated by the results of one or two years' performance. Consider the Mates Investment Fund. This company had bought a substantial number of the shares of Omega Equities, one of the glamorous conglomerates of the mid-sixties. However, it purchased Omega letter stock for only $3.25 per share. (As already indicated, such stock cannot be sold for several years and then only after completing an involved registration procedure with the Securities and Exchange Commission.) The rocketlike market performance of Omega Equities in 1968 helped the Mates Fund to the number-one spot in the mutual fund performance parade for 1968. But in late December, 1968, the Securities and Exchange Commission suspended trading in Omega shares. Accordingly, Mates's fund then lacked any feasible means of determining the value of its own shares. Hence, the fund was granted permission to refuse to redeem these shares. Hence, Mates's shareholders were locked in, unable to exercise their redemption rights for seven months.

Subsequently the value of Omega fell even faster than it had risen. Whereas at the end of 1968 the Mates Fund boasted a net asset value of $15.51 per share, by 1971, after trading in Omega Equities was restored, the net asset value was only $3.56. A 1971 tabulation by the Arthur Lipper Corporation ranked Mates 512 out of a total of 526 funds.

If the past does not provide a sure guide to the future, what else do we have? There seems to be some basis for believing that the fund that has performed better than the average over a long period has developed an investment philosophy and a technique for selecting good stocks that will enable it to continue to do better in the future. For every in-and-out "hot" fund, such as Mates and Enterprise, there are a dozen funds that have shown fairly consistent patterns over the years. Many have 20-year records running through bull and bear markets. We can assess their performance in comparison with the broad market averages as well as with other funds.

The fund's investment objectives must be considered when judging performance. Obviously it is unfair to criticize a failure to make big gains in a bull market if the fund's purpose is to provide steady income from solid preferred stocks and bonds. Neither should you fault a growth fund for its meager 1 percent dividend from operations when it does not aim for dividends. On the other hand, an income fund could be criticized for failing to provide income and failing further to maintain the net asset value of its portfolio. Although investment in a growth fund inherently involves more risk, poor management is indicated when the fund achieves only below-average gains in rising markets and falls more than the average in bear markets.

Before committing yourself to a purchase you should consider your own emotional responses. In theory, growth stocks may be the most sensible investment for the young person with 40 years of earning power ahead. But if the investor is cautious and inclined to worry about the safety of the investment, he or she may be unprepared psychologically for the roller coaster on which growth funds often ride. Of course, the person should hold onto the shares when the market dives in one of its bearish moods. But when the prophets of doom find their way onto the front pages, the investor may begin to fear that the bottom will drop out of the market entirely. At this point theory may not stand a chance against his intense emotional reactions. Similarly, safety of principal may be indicated for the middle-aged couple who will require capital for their retirement, but will they be satisfied with their slow-plodding fund shares that rise a few cents a month while hot-shot funds run up gains in dollars?

It is not sufficient to select the kind of fund most suited to your long-term financial needs; you also must be fairly confident that you will be able to resist the temptation to change your course when it seems that your money will be safer or would produce better profits elsewhere.

Additional Features

Although a fund's ability to achieve its goals is probably the greatest single factor in determining its value, you might also give some weight to those features that only some funds offer. You might want an automatic reinvestment program, the right to reinvest dividends from ordinary income without paying a sales charge. Load funds vary on their position with regard to this, but no-load funds generally do permit it.

Among the services funds provide for shareholders are the following:

Accumulation plans. These plans enable an investor to buy fund shares on a periodic-payment basis. According to the Investment Company Institute, "One of the chief reasons for their popularity is that they offer individuals of modest means an opportunity to build an investment program with relatively small purchases, usually out of current income."

At the end of 1954, when the Investment Company Institute began collecting such statistics, there were 208,295 accumulation plans in force. At the end of 1969, however, the total number of accumulation plans exceeded 4 million.

An accumulation plan enables you to practice dollar-cost averaging. You invest identical amounts of money in shares of a given security at regular intervals. Thus you buy more shares when prices are low and fewer shares when prices are high. The purchase of more shares at lower, rather than higher, prices reduces the average cost of purchases made. In theory at least, it gives you a better chance of minimizing losses and, ultimately, of making a profit.

The "dollar-cost-averaging" plan is based on the idea that it pays to buy if prices drop, for if they rise again, you will have bought at a bargain level. Employing the dollar-cost-averaging plan may serve to reduce the average price you pay per share. It works this way.

Assume that you plan to invest $1,000 every three months for the next 10 years or so. This quarter you put $1,000 into a growth fund and obtain 80 shares worth $12.50 each. (To keep the example simple, we will not take sales commissions into consideration.) By next quarter the price per share has risen to $13.33; thus your $1,000 buys only 75 shares. The following quarter the market has taken a bad spill and the same amount invested buys 85 shares. Later the price has dropped still more, and you get 90 shares for your money. During the year you have obtained 325 shares at an average price of approximately $12.12 per share. By investing the same number of dollars at stated intervals you buy more shares when the price is low. Your average cost per share is less than the average price per share during the same period. Consequently, you stand to profit more if prices rise.

There are two kinds of accumulation plans: voluntary and contractual (*controversial*). Under the voluntary plan you buy shares at regular intervals and pay the full sales charge on each purchase. Thus if you put $500 into a fund every three months, you will pay the maximum sales charge each time.

Under the contractual plan, for example, if you agree to buy $12,000 worth of shares over a ten-year period, you will pay the same sales charge as if you had bought the $12,000 worth at once.

But there's another — and more important — difference. Under the voluntary plan you may discontinue purchases at any time. However, if you have committed yourself to a contractual plan, you have a legal obligation to buy the shares at the agreed intervals. If you breach this contract, you will have to pay higher commission costs.

Automatic investment plans, also known as the Checkomatic plan, is a procedure whereby the shareholder approves the fund spending of a specific sum of money every month for shares. This is an automatic form of dollar averaging. The regular deduction buys a different number of shares each month, depending upon share prices at the time of each purchase. (In authorizing deductions to be made from your checking account, you send the fund a voided personal check that serves as a sample.) Each month a check is drawn on your bank account by the fund and invested in your fund account at the offering price. The canceled checks are returned with your bank statement. You generally can terminate the plan by submitting written notice.

Group investment plans. Some funds waive the minimum requirements for an initial investment and for subsequent purchases of shares when organized groups (sometimes of only 20 or more individuals) join to buy shares through payroll deduction and similar plans. Some load funds offer what is in effect a discount rate: the purchases of all the group members are pooled, and the total is regarded as a single purchase. If the total is large enough, each purchaser pays a lower commission regardless of the size of the purchase.

Automatic reinvestment plans. Instead of taking ordinary and capital gains dividends in cash, you authorize the fund to use the money to buy additional shares for you. Fund representatives paint dramatic pictures of the benefits that accrue to shareholders who reinvest dividends. Robert M. Loeffler, a vice-president of Investors Diversified Services, gave this example at a congressional hearing in 1967:

> If in 1945, when Investors Stock Fund was organized, a customer had invested $1,000 at an 8% sales charge, his total cost would have been $80. By reinvesting his dividends and capital gains distributions at no charge, as 95% of Stock Fund investors do, he would have reduced the effective percentage sales charge on the money he paid in:
>
> At the end of the fifth year he would have paid in a total of

$1,245, and the effective sales charge on the money paid in would have dropped to 6.4%.

At the end of the tenth year he would have paid in $1,939, and the effective sales charges on the money paid in would have dropped to 4.1%.

At the end of the seventeenth year, the usual life of an IDS mutual fund account, he would have paid in $3,547, and the effective sales charge on the money paid in would have dropped to only 2.2%.

At the end of the twenty-second year, October 31, 1966, he would have paid in $5,422, and the effective sales charge on the money paid in would have been less than 1.5%.

In other words, this customer paid a sales charge of $80 to make an initial investment of $1,000 and paid nothing to invest an additional $4,422. If he had then redeemed his shares he would have received $9,558 with no commission charge, all generated from his original $1,000, and the effective charge on all money in and out would have been 0.53%. This is a far cry from an 8% sales load.

Withdrawal plans, in effect, assure you of a certain income each year. Assume that you invest $10,000 in the shares of a fund with such a plan. If it calls for an automatic withdrawal of 6 percent, the investor will be sure of getting $600 a year for an indefinite period. The money will be deducted from dividends due you if the fund's dividends equal or exceed 6 percent. If necessary, the fund will redeem some of the shares to make up the difference between its dividends and the 6 percent payment.

Keogh plans. Many funds offer special pension plans for the self-employed. These plans are named after Representative Eugene Keogh, of Brooklyn, who fought a long battle to give self-employed individuals some of the pension privileges often extended to those who work for others. Under the Keogh plan a self-employer may set aside up to 10 percent of his or her annual income free of present taxes. The self-employer invests this amount in the shares of a fund that has been approved by the Treasury Department. Thereafter, both dividends and capital gains are reinvested and remain free of current taxes. After the person reaches the age of 59, the self-employer may withdraw some or all of his initial contributions plus any gains.

Then the self-employer pays income taxes on the entire amount, but at the rate applicable to his or her income at that time, which presumably is lower during his latter years.

Under a related plan, a self-employed person who has employees may invest as much as an additional 10 percent of taxable income. While the employer must pay income tax on the amount additionally invested, future dividends and capital gains are tax free until that time when he starts taking money out. As required by law, the self-employer's permanent employees who work 20 hours or more a week must be included in the plan.

In 1972 President Nixon proposed that permissible contributions under the Keogh plan be increased. This should make the program even more attractive.

Conversion privilege. This allows you to switch from one fund to another within the same fund group as your needs or objective change. Example: you have invested in a fund for growth of capital for many years. However, now you are retiring and are more interested in current investment income, which is more suitably achieved by an income fund. Usually, conversions are allowed at the cost of the mechanical process of converting an account — often no more than $5.

Pointers for Share Buyers

Be wary of the salesperson who plugs one or two funds exclusively. You are entitled to suspect that the salesperson has self-serving reasons for doing so. Although certain funds will suit your purposes better than others, seldom is the choice limited to those few funds.

When any salesperson (employed by a fund sales organization directly, by a broker-dealer, or by a brokerage house) insists that you should buy shares in one fund only, you should make sure that: (1) the salesperson has thoroughly discussed your financial condition and investment objectives with you; (2) you and the salesperson have agreed upon the kind of fund most likely to help you achieve your objectives; (3) the salesperson has compared the performance records and the managements of the many different funds whose investment objectives fit your own; and (4) you are convinced that the particular fund recommended indeed promises to achieve more for you than competitive funds.

Why adopt such a hard-nosed "show me" attitude? One reason might be that too many inducements exist to tempt a salesperson to sell the fund that serves him or her, not you. When the salesperson concentrates hard-sell efforts on behalf of one fund, it is at least possible that he or she will be rewarded with a more generous commission. If it is a new fund, the commission may be substantially greater. On established funds the salesperson may still get a higher commission rate. If he works for a broker-dealer or brokerage firm, he may get a percentage of the extra commissions earned for executing the fund's buy and sell orders for its portfolio. The fund may be sponsoring an "extra-incentive" campaign, and the salesperson who sells the most shares may enjoy a free two weeks riding the surf at Waikiki. All of these considerations, of course, tend to diminish motivation to provide you with the kind of fund that is best for you.

Some fund publications advise investment not just in one fund but in a package. They argue that diversification is good wherever you get it, that if it makes sense to spread risk among stocks, it also makes sense to spread risk among funds. This argument tends to belittle your ability to choose a fund that will perform better than others. It is true that you may avoid serious mistakes by investing in several funds, for the poor performer may be offset by one that does well. But the reverse is also true: the fund that does well will be dragged down by the laggard. Investing in a number of funds only increases the chance that you will do no better than the stock averages.

The advocates of diversification also advise investing in different kinds of funds. They argue that you should put some of your capital in common stock funds, some in balanced funds consisting of common and preferred stocks and bonds, and some in bond funds. In theory, fixed-income securities will retain their value even if common stock prices sag. Thus you will have greater security than if your investments were limited to common stock funds alone. The reverse is again true, however: when common stock prices move forward, balanced funds are unlikely to join the parade. This approach may provide greater safeguards against catastrophic losses, but it is not likely to realize sizable capital gains. Those who want security would do better to put all of their money in funds the goal of which is to provide security.

If you decide to buy load shares, try to take advantage of the lower sales charges in effect for large-scale purchases. A typical reduction in charges occurs at $25,000. If you invest that amount, you may pay only 6 percent commission, or $1,500. If you had invested only $20,000, on which the load runs $8\frac{1}{2}\%$, you would have paid a total charge of $1,700. It might pay you to borrow $5,000 from your bank to cover the extra purchase. After buying the shares you may sell $5,000 worth to repay the bank; even after the bank deducts its interest charges, you still save $150 or more on what is now a $20,000 purchase. Or you might continue your bank loan, paying it off with additional amounts you had planned to invest in the fund. In this way you will probably save more than $500 in commissions: instead of separate purchases of $20,000 and $5,000 at the top sales commission rate, you make only one purchase of $25,000 at the lower rate.

Funds also charge a lower commission to those who invest more than the breakpoint over a 13-month period. You are entitled to this lower rate if you sign a letter of intent within 90 days of your initial purchase stating that you plan to make these purchases. In such cases the fund usually sets aside a certain number of shares to cover its commission in case you do not fulfill your intention. When you buy enough shares during the period to qualify for the lower commission, these shares are delivered to you. Remember, a letter of intent costs you nothing. If you do not make the intended purchases, you pay no higher commission on shares already bought than you would pay in any event.

What if you have already invested enough to qualify for the breakpoint rate? Sign a letter anyway. It will entitle you to buy additional shares over the 13-month period at the lower commission rate. Assume that you have invested $25,000 at the lowered commission fee of 6 percent. During the next 13 months you put another $5,000 into the fund. With the letter of intent, you pay only 6 percent commission; without it the commission charge would run the full 8½ percent. If you fail to buy more shares during the period, you lose nothing.

Letters of intent accepted by many funds provide for a still lower commission if your purchases reach a breakpoint beyond the one intended. Assume you invest $20,000 in January and plan to invest $5,000 more within 13 months, but in November you find yourself with $30,000 you might use to buy additional shares. You are entitled to the $50,000 breakpoint price rather than the $25,000 price you originally indicated.

When selling fund shares held longer than six months that have appreciated in value, remember that — other things being equal — it is more advantageous to act before dividends from income are declared. By selling before the date on which you become entitled to such dividends you pay only a capital gains tax on the amount of the pay-out. If you sell after that date, the amount of the dividend will be deducted from the price you get per share, but you will face a tax at regular rates on the dividends received.

Switching from one fund to another should never be done without carefully considering all the factors involved. As noted, when you switch from a fund managed by one company to a load fund managed by another, you face a substantial sales charge on your new purchase. In addition, you may have to pay a redemption charge to get out of the first fund; and if you have a gain on those shares, you also face a capital gains tax. A 60-year-old commercial artist had 200 shares of a growth fund worth $3,100, of which $2,100 was profit. His grandnephew, who had just taken a job as a fund salesperson, convinced the artist that he needed security above all else and persuaded his grand-uncle to switch to his employer's income fund. After the artist paid the commission and a capital gains tax of $430, he had only $2,359 to invest in the second fund.

Summing Up: What the Record Shows

This book has suggested that mutual funds are hardly the magic carpet to wealth, as some sponsors suggest. The notion that all investors make big money in mutual funds is, on its face, untenable. The record shows no such thing.

In view of the limitations and defects of other forms of investment, the average person who seeks to hold on to his or her purchasing power and perhaps make it grow is virtually forced into the stock market. An independent investor may find brokers scornful of small orders. Hence such an investor may have to join the many who seek professional management because they know little about the workings of the markets or lack confidence in their ability to make successful choices. Of all the professional money managers, the mutual fund managers operate most openly; and it is at least possible to compare their past performance achievements with those of their competitors and the general market itself. For many, therefore, mutual funds are inevitable.

However, funds remain an imperfect alternative. In their organization, operation, and underlying philosophy, mutual funds leave much to be desired — and much to be corrected. All too frequently the fund becomes an instrument to advance the interests of the management — usually at the shareholders' expense. But the average investor has almost no place else to go. Mutual funds may be a poor vehicle, but for millions of Americans they provide the only wheels in town.

The record does show that, on the average, shareholders in common stock funds in past decades have done better than holders of savings accounts, savings bonds, or gilt-edged bonds, and that these gains were achieved even when the high costs of buying fund shares and the advisory fees charged by fund advisers are taken into account.

The record does not guarantee, of course, that funds will continue to be superior in the future. About that one can only speculate.

The record shows that over the long term, mutual funds on average do no better or worse than stocks in general. While mutual funds may rack up larger gains in bull markets, they also may score larger losses in bear markets. Objective figures suggest that many individuals do as well in managing their own money as the "professionals" do. There is no evidence to prove the extent to which this is so. Nor can hard evidence be found to support the idea that professionals perform better than most individuals in the market. The truth probably is that many persons can do better on their own, but that most individuals lack the time, talent, interest, judgment, and maturity to function successfully in an area where so much is rigged against them.

As numerous SEC and Wharton School studies have shown, the primary advantage of the typical fund is that it shields its shareholders against catastrophic loss. Indeed, on the average, funds perform no better than a representative list of stocks such as those in the Dow-Jones Industrial Average or the Standard and Poor's Composite Index. But the small investor finds it impossible to take a position in all the Dow-Jones or Standard and Poor's stocks. As a practical matter, the investor must concentrate his investments in relatively few issues. These might provide greater gains than the Dow average as a whole, but they also might provide greater losses. Thus the mutual fund coin is two-sided: the fact that fund investments are spread over a large number of stocks means that they generally cannot be expected to do much better than the averages. On the other hand, they will not do much worse.

There are few options available to most investors in protecting and enlarging their assets. The best investment probably is a home of one's own: you enjoy living in it and enjoy seeing its value increase year after year. Most other investment media have built-in hazards. Speculation in real estate has proved profitable for thousands, but it requires large chunks of money that may be tied up for years. When you need cash, you cannot sell a few yards of real estate the way you can a few shares of stock. Savings accounts and savings and other bonds are subject to the ravages of inflation. They may protect the number of your dollars, but they offer little else. Life insurance policies with cash values offer a relatively low return and no protection against a decrease in the dollar's purchasing power.

In view of the limitations and defects of other forms of investment, the average person who seeks to hold on to his or her purchasing power and perhaps make it grow is virtually forced into the stock market. An independent investor may find brokers scornful of small orders. Hence such an investor may have to join the many who seek professional management because they know little about the workings of the markets or lack confidence in their ability to make successful choices. Of all the professional money managers, the mutual fund managers operate most openly; and it is at least possible to compare their past performance achievements with those of their competitors and the general market itself. For many, therefore, mutual funds are inevitable.

However, funds remain an imperfect alternative. In their organization, operation, and underlying philosophy, mutual funds leave much to be desired — and much to be corrected. All too frequently the fund becomes an instrument to advance the interests of the management — usually at the shareholders' expense. But the average investor has almost no place else to go. Mutual funds may be a poor vehicle, but for millions of Americans they provide the only wheels in town.

Appendix:

Where to Get Up-to-Date Information about Funds

Aggressive Growth Funds Report, P. O. Box 667, Los Altos, California 94022. This is a monthly advisory publication specializing in no-load mutual funds. It spotlights the best and poorest market performers among these funds and rates those it considers most attractive on the basis of the fund's intermediate to long-term prospects. It looks for "dynamic, new breed funds" and favors the small but fast-growing ones. The end result is an A,B,C rating geared to more aggressive investors.

Forbes Magazine, 60 Fifth Avenue, New York, New York 10011. A general publication for investors, *Forbes* is published twice monthly. It is sold on newsstands and is also available by subscription. Each issue contains a regular column on investment companies, dealing with developments of specific funds. *Forbes* publishes a mutual fund survey issue every August 15. Included in its tabulations are all publicly distributed funds with total assets of $2 million or more. Easy-to-grasp performance comparisons are given for specific periods of time and for up and down markets.

193

Fund Investment Engineering, Station Square Three, P. O. Box 700, Paoli, Pennsylvania 19301. This service recommends different funds (generally open-ended no-loads) that are performing best at any given time. Its "aggressive growth" package consists of funds selected for exceptional potential; the "conservative growth" portfolio contains diversified funds that have made good gains over a period of years and have shown good down-trend resistance in falling markets. The funds in each package are rated on the basis of their performance at the time of publication in each report. Subscribers are encouraged to move out of funds with lagging performance and into others that are doing better.

FundScope, Suite 700, 1900 Avenue of the Stars, Los Angeles, California 90067. A monthly magazine *FundScope* is the most complete publication dealing with funds available to individual investors. It provides continually updated figures on fund performances, and it issues an annual guide containing the record of each major fund over the past ten years. These data make it possible to compare funds sharing a basic investment objective by contrasting their increases or decreases in asset value, dividends, and capital gains distributions.

FundScope states that it is "not an advisory service. We do not recommend individual funds. We do not give buy/hold/sell advice. Edited from the investor's viewpoint, *FundScope* has no axe to grind for individual funds. *FundScope* tries to be a magazine of facts, not opinions, and lets the record speak for itself." Sample copies are provided upon request.

Growth Fund Guide, P. O. Box 2109, San Clemente, California 92672. This provides an advisory service covering a supervised list of no-load funds. Monthly numerical fund ratings express an opinion on a fund's growth potential. Each fund is given a rating based upon performance, volatility, size, inflow of capital, and management evaluation quotient. The service also publishes personalized performance-rating charts for individual funds, thus allowing for easier comparisons between funds.

Media General Financial Weekly, 119 North Third Street, Richmond, Virginia. Includes — among thousands of statistics on stocks generally — an updating of over 375 mutual fund performance figures. Each issue details the objective of each fund, price per share, distributions from income and capital gains for the current year to date and for the preceding year, present yield, whether the fund is load or no-load, the percentage of assets in cash and equivalents, and the total net assets of the fund as reported in the last quarter.

Mutual Funds Scoreboard, 6 Deer Trail, Old Tappan, New Jersey 07675. This publication is a quarterly report edited by Yale Hirsch, who also edits the highly regarded annual *Mutual Funds Almanac*. The *Scoreboard* shows the percentage gains or losses in assets per share of 564 funds for each quarter and for the preceding year and ranks the funds in order of performance. Each issue also provides news and statistics about the fund industry. The *Scoreboard* and *Almanac* may be purchased separately, but subscribers to the *Scoreboard* may receive the *Almanac* at a reduced rate.

United Business Service, 210 Newbury Street, Boston, Massachusetts 02116. United issues a *Mutual Fund Selector* twice a month, generally on the second and fourth Wednesdays. The first issue of each month includes a statistical survey of over 350 funds and comments on mutual fund performance. The second issue of the month features a supervised list of mutual funds, editorial reports on promising new funds, detailed buying recommendations, and assessments of background fundamentals of the market.

Notes

Chapter 1

1. Securities and Exchange Commission, *Institutional Investor Study Report* (Washington, D.C.: Government Printing Office, 1971, vol. 4), p. 2168.

Chapter 2

1. SEC, *Institutional Investor Study Report*, summary vol. 1, pp. 124-125.
2. *Ibid.*
3. *Ibid.*

Chapter 3

1. Benjamin Graham, David L. Dodd, and Sidney Cottle, *Security Analysis — Principles and Techniques*, 4th ed. rev. (New York: McGraw-Hill, 1962), p. 425.
2. *Ibid.*, pp. 740-741.

197

3. SEC, *Study of Mutual Funds* (Washington, D.C.: Government Printing Office, 1962).

4. Irwin Friend, Marshal E. Blume, and Jean Crockett, *Mutual Funds and Other Institutional Investors: A New Perspective* (New York: McGraw-Hill, 1970).

5. *Ibid.*, pp. 52-56.

6. White Plains (N.Y.) *Reporter-Dispatch*, 5 January 1971, p. 11.

7. U.S. Congress House, Subcommittee on Commerce and Finance of the Committee on Interstate and Foreign Commerce, *Hearings on Investment Company Act Amendments of 1967* (Washington, D.C.: Government Printing Office, 1970), part 1, pp. 204-207.

8. "Rates of Return on Investments in Common Stock: The Year-by-Year Record, 1926-1965," *Journal of Business of the University of Chicago,* July, 1968, reprinted, Merrill Lynch, Pierce, Fenner and Smith, Inc.

9. *Forbes*, 15 July 1971, p. 64.

10. Friend, Blume, and Crockett, *Mutual Funds and Other Institutional Investors*, pp. 16-17.

11. *Ibid.*, p. 66.

12. *New York Times*, 3 September 1970, sec. 3, p. 10.

13. SEC, *Institutional Investor Study Report*, summary vol. 1, p. 151.

14. *Ibid.*, p. 102.

15. *Ibid.*

16. George J. W. Goodman, "Performance is the Name of the Game," *The Anatomy of Wall Street* (New York: Award Books, 1968), p. 72.

17. *Ibid.*

18. Friend, Blume, and Crockett, *Mutual Funds and Other Institutional Investors*, pp. 66-67.

19. SEC, *Report on the Public Policy Implications of Investment Company Growth* (Washington, D.C.: Government Printing Office, 1966), p. 257.

20. *Ibid.*, pp. 256-257.

21. *Forbes,* 15 September 1971, pp. 43-44.

22. U.S. Congress House, *Investment Company Act Amendments of 1967*, part 1, pp. 36-37.

23. SEC, *Institutional Investor Study Report*, supp. vol. 1, p. 230.

24. *Ibid.*

25. SEC, *Public Policy Implications of Investment Company Growth*, p. 252.

26. *Wall Street Journal*, 24 February 1971, p. 1.

27. *Ibid.*

28. *Ibid.*, 11 March 1971, p. 24.

29. R. E. Diefenbach, "How Good Is Institutional Brokerage Research?" *Financial Analysts Journal*, January-February, 1972, pp. 54-60.

30. *New York Times*, 9 January 1970, p. 52.

31. *Fortune*, April, 1969, p. 81.

32. Bradbury K. Thurlow, "Contrary Opinion Theory: The Psychological Approach," *The Anatomy of Wall Street* (New York: Award Books, 1968), p. 245.

33. John Maynard Keynes, *The General Theory of Employment, Interest and Money* (New York: Harcourt, Brace, 1936) p. 156.

34. *New York Times*, 29 January 1970, p. 32.

Chapter 4

1. SEC, *Public Policy Implications of Investment Company Growth*, p. 46.

2. *Ibid.*, p. 65.

3. *Ibid.*, p. 72.

4. U.S. Congress House, *Hearings on Investment Company Act Amendments of 1967*, part 1, p. 40.

5. U.S. Congress House, Subcommittee on Commerce and Finance of the Committee on Interstate and Foreign Commerce, *Hearings on Mutual Fund Amendments* (Washington, D.C.: Government Printing Office, 1970), pp. 854-855.

6. U.S. Congress House, *Hearings on Investment Company Act Amendments of 1967*, part 1, p. 34.

7. U.S. Congress House, *Hearings on Mutual Fund Amendments*, part 2, p. 788.

8. U.S. Congress Senate, Committee on Banking and Currency, Hearing on S.1659 (Washington, D.C.: Government Printing Office, 1967), p. 696.

9. U.S. Congress House, *Hearings on Mutual Fund Amendments*, part 2, p. 788.

10. U.S. Congress House, *Hearings on Investment Company Act Amendments of 1967*, part 2, pp. 686-697.
11. *Ibid.*, p. 698.
12. *Ibid.*, p. 820.
13. SEC, *Institutional Investor Study Report*, summary vol. 1, pp. 27-28.
14. U.S. Congress House, *Hearings on Investment Company Act Amendments of 1967*, part 1, pp. 41-42.
15. *Ibid.*, part 1, p. 36.
16. *Ibid.*, part 1, p. 31.
17. *Ibid.*
18. *Ibid.*, part 2, pp. 693-694.
19. U.S. Congress House, *Hearings on Mutual Fund Amendments*, part 2, p. 872.
20. SEC, *Institutional Investor Study Report*, vol. 4, pp. 2277-2278.
21. *Ibid.*, summary vol. 1, p. 108.
22. U.S. Congress House, *Hearings on Mutual Fund Amendments*, part 1, p. 209.
23. SEC, *Public Policy Implications of Investment Company Growth*, pp. 149-150.
24. *New York Times*, 1 October 1971, p. 57.

Chapter 5

1. Louis Engel, *How to Buy Stocks*, 4th ed. rev. (New York: Bantam Books, 1968), p. 149.
2. U.S. Congress House, *Hearings on Investment Company Act Amendments of 1967*, p. 655.
3. U.S., Congress House, Committee on Interstate and Foreign Commerce, *Hearings on Investment Company Act Amendments of 1970* (Washington, D.C.: Government Printing Office, 1970), p. 75.
4. SEC, *Report of Special Study of Securities Markets* (Washington, D.C.: Government Printing Office, 1963), part 4, p. 117.
5. *Ibid.*, p. 114.
6. *Ibid.*
7. *Ibid.*, p. 115.
8. *Ibid.*, pp. 128-129.
9. *Ibid.*, p. 129.

10. *Ibid.*, pp. 167-168.
11. *Ibid.*
12. *Ibid.*, pp. 207-208.
13. *Ibid.*, p. 340.
14. *Ibid.*, pp. 343-345.
15. *Ibid.*, p. 345.
16. *Ibid.*, p. 348.
17. *Ibid.*, pp. 208-209.
18. *Ibid.*, p. 209.
19. U.S. Congress House, *Hearings on Investment Company Act Amendments of 1967*, part 2, pp. 651-653.
20. *Ibid.*, pp. 441-442.

Chapter 6

1. SEC, *Special Study of Securities Markets*, part 4, p. 241.
2. *Ibid.*, p. 253.
3. U.S. Congress House, *Hearings on Mutual Fund Amendments*, part 2, p. 814.
4. SEC, Administrative Proceeding, File No. 3-1004.
5. *Ibid.*
6. SEC, Administrative Proceeding, File No. 3-1680.
7. *Fortune*, December, 1969, pp. 163-168.
8. *Ibid.*, p. 168.
9. U.S. Congress House, *Hearings on Investment Company Act Amendments of 1967*, part 2, p. 742.
10. *Forbes*, 1 July 1971, p. 55.
11. *Wall Street Journal*, 1 February 1968, p. 1.
12. U.S. Congress House, *Hearings on Investment Company Act Amendments of 1967*, part 1, p. 182.
13. *New York Times*, 14 October 1971, p. 66.
14. U.S. Congress House, *Hearings on Mutual Fund Amendments*, p. 815.
15. *Wall Street Journal*, 1 February 1968, p. 1.
16. U.S. Congress House, *Hearings on Mutual Fund Amendments*, part 2, pp. 816-817.
17. Louis Engel, *How to Buy Stocks*, 4th ed. rev. (New York: Bantam Books, 1968), p. 152.

THE MUTUAL FUND TRAP

Chapter 7

1. U.S. Congress House, *Hearings on Investment Company Act Amendments of 1967*, part 2, pp. 691-706.
2. SEC, *Institutional Investor Study Report*, vol. 2, p. 372.
3. *FundScope*, January, 1971, p. 77.

Chapter 8

1. Gerald M. Loeb, *The Battle for Investment Survival* (New York: Simon and Schuster, 1965), p. 169.
2. *Fortune*, October, 1971, p. 73.
3. *Ibid.*
4. SEC, *Institutional Investor Study Report*, vol. 1, p. 124.
5. *Fortune*, April, 1969, p.
6. SEC, *Public Policy Implications of Investment Company Growth*, pp. 256-263.
7. U.S. Congress House, *Hearings on Investment Company Act Amendments of 1967*, p. 466.

Index